HAUNTED
CEMETERIES
OF INDIANA

HAUNTED CEMETERIES OF INDIANA

ASHLEY HOOD

Haunted America

Published by Haunted America
A Division of The History Press
Charleston, SC
www.historypress.com

Front cover: courtesy of Elizabeth Christjansen.
Back cover: courtesy of Elizabeth Christjansen; *inset*: courtesy of Elizabeth Christjansen.

All images are courtesy of Elizabeth Christjansen.

First published 2020

Manufactured in the United States

ISBN 9781467146715

Library of Congress Control Number: 2020938503

The cemetery is an open space among the ruins, covered in winter with violets and daisies. It might make one in love with death, to think that one should be buried in so sweet a place.
—*Percy Bysshe Shelley, Adonais*

CONTENTS

CONTENTS

ACKNOWLEDGEMENTS

I have to start by thanking Elizabeth Christjansen, my friend and a wonderful photographer, without whom there would be no pictures in this book. Thank you for once again braving the Indiana winter with me and taking some truly fantastic photos of Indiana's cemeteries. I promise that the next time around, we'll visit some warm and toasty indoor locations.

I also have to thank Stephanie Tyler for her willingness to venture out to haunted locations with me and for always being open-minded to the existence of the supernatural. On the flip side of that, thank you to my dad, Greg Cesinger, for always being a skeptic and reminding me that there can sometimes be a natural cause for the things I experience, especially when visiting cemeteries.

A big thank-you to Howard Wooden for words of encouragement and always reminding me that the history of the locations I visit is just as important as the stories of the spirits that remain there.

Lastly, I have to express great gratitude to all of the people who tend to and care for cemeteries, be it the archivists, the landscapers, the tombstone cleaners or the people who volunteer their time to pick up trash. Without you, the gravestones might crumble and the history and the lives of those buried in Indiana's cemeteries and graveyards might be lost forever. Thank you again for all you do.

Introduction

T he Hoosier State is often associated with cornfields and auto racing, and though it may not be the first place you think of when it comes to ghosts and hauntings, people have been traveling to Indiana since the first Native Americans inhabited the area as early as 8000 BC; cemeteries have dotted the landscape since that time. Indiana currently has about one hundred thousand cemeteries and burial grounds. Some are massive and ornate, almost park-like, while others lie forgotten, in deep forests or along overgrown riverbanks. Some have even been lost entirely, only to be found when urban progress unearths the remains of an old burial ground or family cemetery. But these graveyards and cemeteries often have one thing in common: they tend to be hauntingly beautiful places regardless of their condition.

My interest in the spirits of Indiana's cemeteries and graveyards stems from adventures as a middle-schooler to go "spooking" with my mom. She was quite versed in the lore of Clay and Vigo Counties in Indiana, so we would venture out to local cemeteries to see if we could catch a glimpse of anything out of the ordinary. At the time, we had no fancy equipment, save for an old 110 camera and, later, a 35mm camera. But the spark had been lit. In the years since, I have been able to expand my knowledge of the paranormal and also to visit some well-known haunted locations. But my interest in the "ghost stories" of Indiana's cemeteries and graveyards has always remained. Since that time, my cemetery research has expanded beyond the ghostly residents that may inhabit these locations. Cemeteries have a unique ability to not only keep alive the history of those buried there but also offer a glimpse into the history of a specific city or town and, sometimes, even events that were important to an area.

As a paranormal investigator, I am well aware that many in the field do not give much credence to ghostly activity in cemeteries. This is mostly because many believe that ghosts haunt places that they were familiar with in life, such as their former residences, businesses or locations where they may have spent a great deal of time. For the most part, I agree with this. However, I cannot discount the many tales of ghostly activity reported in cemeteries. Some of these stories involve former graveyard or mortuary employees, grieving family members or, in some instances, events that occurred on the land before the first burial plot was placed there.

Early on in my research, I found that Indiana actually has more haunted cemeteries than I expected—so many, in fact, that I can't possibly cover them all here. In selecting the cemeteries to focus on, I tried to choose locations with a long history of burials and numerous reported accounts of paranormal activity through the years. I visited several cemeteries in each of the three regions of Indiana: northern, central and southern. By doing this, I hope readers can use this book as a roadmap of sorts when exploring Indiana's cemeteries, for both paranormal investigations and historical purposes. Before undertaking my adventures to the haunted cemeteries of Indiana, I researched the history and reported paranormal activity of each cemetery as well as the area of Indiana where the cemetery is located. I also attempted to find historical evidence to support the reported ghostly activity and, in some cases, to give the spirits an identity and perhaps tie them to specific people buried in the cemetery. During this tour of Indiana's cemeteries, I will also feature some of the strange and bizarre tales, true crimes and urban legends that can be found within these hallowed grounds.

I hope that, after reading the supernatural tales of Indiana's cemeteries, you, too, feel compelled to go out and visit some of the locations for yourself. However, I must stress that it is never okay to trespass in cemeteries after hours. And, when visiting, please be as respectful as possible and always remember that cemeteries and graveyards serve as eternal homes for the dead, not only in this life but also possibly in their afterlife.

Happy haunting!

PART I
NORTHERN INDIANA

1

EWALD CEMETERY (LITTLE EGYPT CEMETERY)

FIFTH ROAD, BREMEN, IN 46506
MARSHALL COUNTY
HOURS: DAWN UNTIL DUSK

Ewald Cemetery—or Little Egypt, as it is more commonly known—is a horror movie–esque little cemetery in the rural farmlands of Bremen, Indiana. It is hidden away on what feels like a dirt path but is actually a road that winds tightly around the cemetery before continuing onward to a well-known Bremen legend called the Troll Bridge. It is a story very much in the vein of the "Three Billy Goats Gruff," only quite a bit more terrifying. There are just over one hundred burials on the grounds of Little Egypt, though one would not know it, as the cemetery has been highly vandalized through the years. No more than thirty tombstones remain. In an attempt to curb the damage to the cemetery, a small fence was erected with barbed wire at the top. But this has not stopped vandals from attempting to enter the area, as large holes are visible on both the front and back sides of the fence, leaving the cemetery once again vulnerable to ravagers. Due to this, the area is routinely policed at night, and trespassers are asked to leave.

The cemetery takes the name *Ewald* from three children who are buried there. Jacob and Barbara Ewald had twelve children; unfortunately, not all of them grew into adulthood. Newborn Matilda passed away on September 20, 1865. She was followed to the other side by her four-year-old brother, Henry, on October 9, 1870, and her four-year-old sister, Catherine,

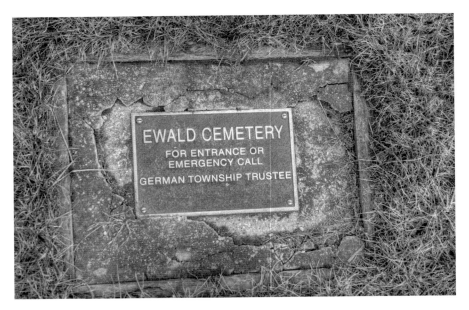

Plaque at Ewald/Little Egypt Cemetery.

Poem on the grave of John Miller at Little Egypt Cemetery.

on March 24, 1873. Of the three siblings, only a piece of Catherine's tombstone remains today.

The first burial in Little Egypt was also that of a child, eight-year-old Alfred Knobloch. Sadly, he was joined by his sister Elnora just a few months later, on March 29, 1853. As with two of the Ewald children, there is no evidence of Alfred and Elnora's tombstones in the cemetery. When wandering around Little Egypt, one might notice the fragments of a small stone, broken and battered, with just a poem left. This, too, is the grave of a child. His name is John Miller, and he passed away a day after his second birthday, on May 12, 1856. It might seem strange for so many children to end up buried in such a small cemetery, but this was an era when contagious diseases were very hard to control. Young children were particularly susceptible, especially those in rural communities. However, the children of Little Egypt are not alone. They are joined by several German immigrants-turned-farmers as well as soldiers who served with the 22nd, 29th, 73rd and 155th Indiana Infantries during the Civil War.

The remote location of Little Egypt has made it a hot spot for teenagers and amateur ghost hunters alike due to the many spooky stories associated with the site. For those from the northern part of the state, Little Egypt is

Weathered tombstone at Little Egypt Cemetery.

likely a location they became familiar with due to campfire tales and stories passed around at family gatherings. Accounts of satanic activity on the grounds have also long circulated, causing many to claim that Little Egypt is truly a frightening place and that, perhaps, the stain of satanic worship has left its mark on the site and could be to blame for much of the paranormal activity on the grounds.

One of the most prevalent stories seems to focus on one of the many children's graves at Little Egypt. Depending on the version of the story you hear, if you leave a nickel or a quarter on one particular infant's grave, you will immediately hear the sound of a crying baby. Apparently, the young soul passed away as a result of choking on a coin. Again, depending on which version of the story you've been told, the crying will emanate from beneath the ground, just below your feet or from very close by in the cemetery. Other accounts, however, state that one does not have to leave a coin to hear the cries of a child and that the sound is actually quite a frequent occurrence on the grounds. Small handprints have also been witnessed on the windows of vehicles, leaving many to wonder if the ghostly children were trying to hitch a ride to the last place they called home.

The angry spirit of a farmer has also been reported by many visitors to Little Egypt. As the story goes, he had a farm not far from the cemetery. One day, while doing work in one of his fields, he was involved in some sort of accident that resulted in his death. His body was interred at Little Egypt, and it wasn't long before nighttime thrill seekers reported encounters with the farmer. His glowing apparition is said to rise from the field and chase trespassers from the cemetery grounds before once again disappearing. However, the farmer is not the only spirit reported to protect the hallowed grounds of Little Egypt. Reports of a phantom vehicle have long circulated, with many people claiming to have had run-ins with the vehicle. Most stories share similar details, in that visitors to the cemetery will see headlights in a nearby field. The car seems to move toward the cemetery at a much faster speed than a vehicle should be able to on rough and uneven farm ground. By the time the visitors are back in their car and accelerating out of the cemetery, they will see the phantom vehicle in their rearview mirror. Many report that it appears to be a large, older-model black sedan. It will keep pace with those fleeing from the cemetery until they cross the Troll Bridge, at which time the sedan seems to just disappear.

Shadowy apparitions have been witnessed moving among the tombstones and on the grounds outside of the fence. One ghostly figure in particular has given many visitors quite a shock. It is said that as you approach the cemetery and it becomes visible in your headlights, the spirit of a young man will run directly in front of your vehicle. His skin appears white as a sheet, and he seems to be running from something. Drivers will often slam on their brakes to avoid hitting the man, but once they step out of the car to check on him, he is nowhere to be found. When taking photographs at night, many people have reported capturing images containing orbs or strange mists that were not visible to the naked eye at the time. Reports of bloodstains appearing on a tree in the cemetery have also long circulated, as have stories of a man's voice being heard by visitors to Little Egypt. Sometimes, the voice sounds as if it is trying to speak; at other times, it is reported as an agonizing groan. While it is not recommended that you visit Little Egypt at night, it is certainly an interesting, albeit unsettling location to explore during the day. But please remember to be respectful, as the spectral inhabitants of the area have seen enough damage and vandalism on the grounds to last them their entire afterlife.

2

TILLETT CEMETERY

1262–1296 East Lovers Lane Road, Peru, IN 46970
Miami County
Hours: Dawn until dusk

Tillett Cemetery is located near an RV dealership and an industrial park but could easily be missed. It is hidden at the top of a forested hill with only a steep dirt path allowing access to the cemetery. There are about 150 interments on the grounds, but only a handful of tombstones remain, many of which are illegible or broken. The area first served as a rural cemetery for the Tillett family, thus giving the cemetery its name. However, this was so long ago that there is currently no record of the identity of the Tilletts buried on the grounds. Instead, the first burial recorded was that of John M. Porter on December 18, 1819. His stone is one of many that are now absent from the grounds.

Tillett Cemetery is also the final resting place of many members of the Banks family, including Augustus Banks, who, after arriving in Peru, Indiana, in 1837, worked at the *Peru Forester*, a weekly newspaper. He worked there until its closure in January 1839 and then became the editor of the *Peru Gazette*, a Saturday newspaper published from July 20, 1839, to April 16, 1842. He is also credited with helping establish the earliest version of the *Miami County Sentinel*. After his retirement, he spent most of his time at his farm and lived a rather quiet life. He passed away at the age of ninety on January 23, 1891. He shares a battered and broken stone with his wife,

Tillett Cemetery sign.

Sarah, who died on December 31, 1894. They are joined in the cemetery by two of their three children, sons John and David. Their daughter, Martha, is buried in Mount Greenwood Cemetery in Chicago, Illinois.

The grave of John Reece has quite a sorrowful story to tell. John had moved to Peru from North Carolina with his wife in the mid-1800s. He immediately befriended a man named Joseph Tillett, likely a descendant of the Tilletts' buried in the cemetery. The two men often spent time together, so John was heartbroken when, on April 30, 1880, Joseph was struck and killed by a train in Peru. It is said that John was dispirited from the death of this close friend and was never quite the same afterward. On December 2, 1880, there were reports of another person being struck by a train in Peru, with the engineer stating that just after 12:35 a.m., he saw a man approach the tracks and lie down. The engineer applied the brakes, hoping to avoid hitting the man. Unfortunately, the engine passed over the man before the train came to a halt. When authorities arrived, they found the head of John Reece lying between the rails; his body was just off the side of the track. He was buried in Tillett Cemetery not long after. Interestingly, Joseph Tillett was originally buried in Tillett Cemetery, likely not far from where John Reece was laid to rest, reuniting the friends in death. Joseph's remains were later moved to Peru's Reyburn Cemetery for reasons unknown.

Fallen tombstone at Tillett Cemetery.

Broken tombstone at Tillett Cemetery.

Tillett Cemetery is one of the many locations across the United States associated with the urban legend of the Hookman. In this case, the story states that the Hookman was a serial killer who lost his hand and replaced it with a grisly hook. He hunted his victims, often couples, on Lovers Lane, just down the hill from Tillett Cemetery. When the Hookman died, he was buried first in Tillett Cemetery but was later moved into the woods and away from the other inhabitants on the grounds. His grave is reportedly on private property now and reachable only on foot. In the years since his death, local teenagers have often been warned to stay away from Lovers Lane because the spirit of the Hookman is known to frequent the area on foggy nights looking for his next victim or victims. Due to this myth, many refer to the area as Hookman Hill.

The cemetery is also home to its fair share of ghostly activity. Many visitors claim that the hill is often blanketed in a deep, low fog that sometimes obscures the remaining gravestones from view. It is said that this fog occurs even during the day. According to one legend, if you drive around the cemetery three times and come to a stop at the bottom of the hill, you will witness skulls rolling down out of the fog and your car will not start. Other reported activity includes cold spots and disembodied voices throughout the cemetery and mists that seem to take on a human-like shape. Photographs taken on the grounds reveal orbs and one tombstone that seems to glow green, although this is never seen with the naked eye. Visitors also report the feeling of being watched and an entity that is known to be rather aggressive, often chasing people down the hill and away from the cemetery. One thing is certain: even if the Hookman does not haunt Tillett Cemetery, many believe that paranormal activity is a common occurrence there and that some of the spectral inhabitants do not rest easy in their graves.

3

MOUNT HOPE CEMETERY

1800 GRANT STREET, LOGANSPORT, IN 46947
CASS COUNTY
HOURS: DAILY FROM 8:00 A.M. TO 4:00 P.M.
WEBSITE: HTTP://WWW.CITYOFLOGANSPORT.ORG/DEPARTMENTS/CEMETERY

Mount Hope Cemetery is reported to be the third-largest cemetery in the state of Indiana, with nearly eighty-one thousand interments across roughly two hundred acres. The cemetery was established in 1857, with the first burial being that of a Mr. Benjamin Peters, who died on May 2, 1857. His tombstone memorializes his status as the first interment on the grounds with an inscription stating just that. Mount Hope is the final resting place of two congressmen and three senators, all serving during the 1800s or early 1900s. The best known of the five politicians is likely Brigadier General John Tipton. He served during the War of 1812 and later became sheriff of Harrison County, as well as being elected to the positions of congressman and senator. He passed away from "a brief illness due to exposure to inclement weather" on April 5, 1839, just two short months after the death of his second wife, Matilda. They were both initially buried in the Spencer Cemetery, but when Spear and Ninth Streets connected there, the graves were moved to the Old Ninth Street Cemetery. However, this would not be the couple's place of eternal rest for long. They were later moved to Mount Hope, where a large monument now stands for both of them. Logansport was also one of many cities in

Lamb sculpture on a tombstone at Mount Hope Cemetery.

Indiana affected by the building of the Erie Canal. Many families moved to the area because of the work that the canal brought. Unfortunately, not long after construction began, there was a malaria outbreak among the workers, with many succumbing to the disease. The bodies were originally buried in an area on the east side of the old Ninth Street Cemetery, not far from Mount Hope. But when a road project was planned that would cut through that section of the Ninth Street grounds, some of the bodies had to be moved, including those from the malaria epidemic. The city decided that the best course of action was to move the bodies to Mount Hope, though records indicating who was disinterred and when are rather difficult to find. The move was completed, but it is not clear if this was the same road project that caused General and Mrs. Tipton to be moved to Mount Hope as well.

Mount Hope Cemetery is a stunning example of Victorian Gothic mortuary design, with many of the tombstones and mausoleums having been influenced by the Victorian architecture throughout the city. Mount Hope is also home to many monuments influenced by the art deco movement. Others feature neoclassical elements. The most unique of the structures in the cemetery are two mausoleums that greet visitors as they enter the main gate. They are built into the hillside and incorporate both Gothic and

Italianate design with vaulted ceilings and exposed brick. They are somewhat reminiscent of something you might see in a Tim Burton movie. The mausoleums are nearly identical. One belongs to the Crismonds, the other to the Murdocks. It seems that besides twin mausoleums, the only other thing that the families have in common are two sisters; Annette Himmelberger Murdock, the wife of William Owens Murdock, and Lillie Himmelberger Crismond, the wife of Horace J. Crismond. The Himmelberger girls were the daughters of local Cass County sheriff Isaac Himmelberger. Annette died on March 14, 1904, at the age of twenty-eight. Her remains were interred in the Murdock mausoleum. Her husband, William, is buried elsewhere in Mount Hope, in the family plot of his second wife, Harriett S. Sewell, sharing a stone with Harriet and her brother and his wife, leaving Annette alone in the Murdock mausoleum. Annette's sister Lillie lived to be eighty-six, but rather than be buried in the family mausoleum with her husband, Horace Crismond, who had preceded her in death, she instead chose to be interred in the Himmelberger family mausoleum at Mount Hope along with her daughter, Kathryn Crismond Armacost, and parents, Isaac and Catherine Himmelberger. Lillie's husband is joined in his mausoleum by his two young grandchildren, Richard Armacost, not quite one year old, and Jeanette Armacost, age seven. They are both the children of Kathryn Armacost Crismond. Also interred in the Crismond mausoleum are Dr. John Crismond, Horace's brother, and Arthur Grund, Horace's son-in-law. Arthur's birth and death years have been inscribed incorrectly on the mausoleum, stating that he was born in 1893 and passed away in 1923. Actually, he was born in 1890 and passed away in 1922. One can't help but wonder how such an erroneous mistake was made, considering that the engraving would have likely been placed on the mausoleum at the time of his death.

With so many of Mount Hope's early burials coming from the upper class of society, it is no wonder that some went to extremes to protect the bodies of their family members from grave robbers, also known as "Resurrectionists" or "Graveyard Ghouls." One such story comes from December 15, 1939, when gravediggers in Mount Hope accidently came across a "Grave Bomb or Grave Torpedo" in an unmarked plot that was not in cemetery records. A grave bomb was a device supplied by mortuaries at the time to protect the remains of the deceased from being stolen in the dark of night. The bomb had double hammers that were attached to powder springs. These hammers were attached to firing pins by thin wires that were stretched across the entire lid of the coffin. If a grave robber should tamper

Crismond and Murdock mausoleums at Mount Hope Cemetery.

with the burial plot, their shovel strikes would quite likely sever the wires, causing the hammers to strike the firing pins, resulting in an explosion. While no one is certain what mortuary may have placed the bomb at Mount Hope, it seemed to be attached to one of the older graves in the Huntley-Orwin plot, likely dating to 1885. The bomb, which was thought to be inactive due to its age, had initially been given to the family that owned the plot, but they turned it over to the newly formed Indiana State Police, which at the time had been active for only six years. Lieutenant Don Franklin, an early explosives expert, drilled a hole in the bomb's casing to remove some of the black powder for testing. The results showed that, though the powder had lost most of its strength, it was still dry and likely could have been ignited. This same bomb is now on display at the Cass County Historical Society in Logansport. Apparently, these bombs were somewhat common, and larger cemeteries often kept records of which burials might be armed. But this was not so common in smaller cemeteries, provoking the question, how many grave torpedoes might still be underground today?

Mount Hope is also known for the unusual inscriptions that adorn many of the mausoleums and tombstones on the grounds. Some include literary quotes from well-known plays and fairytales, such as *Hamlet* and *Hansel and Gretel*. Others have quotes such as, "Knock three times and they shall

Tombstones with literary quotes at Mount Hope Cemetery.

Inscription on tombstone at Mount Hope Cemetery.

come." Considering that some of the mausoleums are embellished with door knockers that one can actually use, that quote is somewhat more ominous, especially considering that the cemetery is said to have its share of paranormal activity.

The most common reported occurrence seems to be the sound of horses throughout the cemetery, with visitors reporting not only the sound of hooves against the ground but also neighing and whinnying. Canon fire has reportedly been recorded as electronic voice phenomena, or EVP, as well as the sounds of what seem to be grunting and gurgling. The cemetery is home to the Veteran's Circle, an area devoted to the burials of those who have served in the United States military. Knowing that this area exists in the cemetery makes one wonder if perhaps there could be residual haunting on the grounds, possibly associated with the experiences of those in the Veteran's Circle. Mist-like apparitions have been witnessed on the grounds, and some visitors have reported feeling as though they have been touched by someone when no one is nearby. People have also reported someone frequently being heard whistling on the grounds, and if they whistle back, the unseen soul will often respond. Perhaps the best way to confirm the ghostly activity at Mount Hope is to take a stroll through the grounds, being sure to keep your ears open for any spirited sounds.

4

JUSTUS CEMETERY (SOUTH CEMETERY)

805 SOUTH HOWARD STREET, OXFORD, IN 47971
BENTON COUNTY
HOURS: DAWN UNTIL DUSK

Justus Cemetery is located not far from the wind farms of Fowler, in Oxford, a town best known for Dan Patch, the famous racehorse. The cemetery, well maintained and quiet, has just under twelve hundred interments. There may be more, however. Some of the graves at the site may not have been recorded or in some cases were left unmarked, as burials have occurred there since 1808. The ground was established as a proper cemetery in 1840 and still includes the original iron gate. The gate is no longer in use, as a gravel drive now circles the entire grounds. The first burial was that of James McConnell, who passed away on March 11, 1840.

One notable grave on the grounds belongs to a thirteen-year-old boy, Carol Albertson, who died attempting to save the lives of others on June 2, 1938. His grave can be found in the west division, row nine, column J. Carol had been fishing at a pond with fellow thirteen-year-old Marvin Mounce. Marvin's mother, Madge, and his twelve-year-old sister, Colleen, were also nearby. His sister was wading in the shallow water, unaware that her next step would be deadly. As Colleen waded, she stepped into a steep drop-off, disappearing beneath the water. Madge's terrified screams brought the boys running, with Marvin jumping straight in after his sister. Carol, aware that Marvin could not swim, attempted to use a pole to bring the two children

Original gate at Justus Cemetery.

to shore. In the process, he, too, was pulled into the deep water. Both boys disappeared into the abyss. Colleen had managed to surface at that point and was assisted to the shore by terrified onlookers who had now formed around the pond. The bodies of both boys were recovered, and their funerals were held together at the Albertson family home. Marvin is buried with his parents at the Boswell Cemetery in Boswell, Indiana.

Though there are only a few modern reports of paranormal activity in Justus Cemetery, it is often regarded as having one of the spookiest tales of any location in the state. As with all good ghost stories, this one begins on a dark and stormy night. A steam locomotive was passing through on its way along the Chicago and Eastern Illinois Railroad when a stop for water was required. The tower stood not far from Justus Cemetery, no doubt an ominous sight in such foul weather. As the railroad employees exited the train to collect the water, the task was immediately interrupted by a sorrowful moan that cut through the rain and seemed to be emanating from within the water tower. The sound was so loud that even the passengers on the train took note that something wasn't right. No one had to wait long for the source to reveal itself. According to accounts, a glowing white apparition seemed to hover above the water tower before slowly floating toward the train. The workers hurried their pace and quickly returned

Grave of Carol Albertson at Justus Cemetery.

with the water, while everyone on board braced themselves for otherworldly contact. Just as it seemed that the spirit would join them on the train, it changed its path, drifting toward Justus Cemetery before disappearing into an open grave. The train chugged on, but the experience left the workers dreading their next visit to the water tower.

A few days after the initial incident, the same train—with the exception of a few crew members who had been too frightened to return to the route—was once again chugging its way through the area and stopped at the tower. Everything seemed to go off without a hitch, and the apparition that had haunted them previously was nowhere to be seen. As the engineer brought the train to life, he could tell something wasn't right; the engine was frozen in place as if it was being held there by an unseen force. As the panicked crew began weighing their options—either stay on board or flee into the cemetery—the train broke loose and continued down the track. After some discussion, the workers decided that they would no longer make stops at the water tower. This decision concerned the train company, which opted to hire a detective to investigate the situation. This seemed to put the crew members' minds at ease, and after a few days, they decided to resume stops at the water tower.

The detective, having been made aware of the train's next scheduled stop, rallied a few brave townspeople to join him to observe the locomotive's arrival. As the party arrived and began to wander the area, a member of the group noticed some teenage boys loitering near the water tower. The detective considered the activity suspicious. After corralling the boys, it was discovered that they had a white sheet in their possession. After a bit of prodding, the teenagers admitted to using a wire attached to the water tower to make the sheet appear to come alive. As for the unseen force that held the train, it was soap on the tracks, according to the youths. Though this certainly closed the case in the mind of the detective, many of the crew members as well as local citizens remained unconvinced and believed that supernatural forces had, indeed, been at play.

Tombstones at Justus Cemetery.

In the years since this story gained attention, some have ventured to Justus Cemetery in an attempt to have a one-on-one encounter with the entity, with many visitors leaving the grounds disappointed. There has been the occasional report of strange activity on the grounds, but this is limited mostly to orbs and the occasional EVP. It seems as though Justus Cemetery is one location that deserves a more in-depth look. Could there be any truth to the reports of ghostly activity, or is the cemetery's reputation just a result of a decades-old prank that doesn't seem to want to die?

5

POSEY CHAPEL CEMETERY

3789 East County Road 1000 North, La Porte, IN 46350
La Porte County
Hours: Dawn until dusk

Posey Chapel Cemetery is located on a small rolling hill with beautiful views of the landscape around it. The land was originally owned by an early settler, Wightman Goit. In 1833, he allowed some of his land to be used for the growing Methodist congregation in the area, with a small log building being erected on the grounds of the present-day Posey Chapel Cemetery. In 1838 and 1839, Goit allowed for the burial of two children, Thomas and Lucetta Sutherland-Foster, on the grounds near the church. He may have also allowed for other burials on the site, but no records currently exist. Following the burials of the Sutherland-Foster children, it would be a few more years before a proper cemetery was located at the site.

In 1841, a gentleman named Wade Posey moved to the area and quickly joined the Methodist community. It wasn't long after his arrival that Posey attempted to convince the congregation that a new chapel was needed for religious services. Many people agreed. The new log chapel was finished in November 1842 and christened Posey Chapel, after Wade Posey. With so many residents now attending services at Posey Chapel, it made sense to expand the small cemetery beyond the interments already on the grounds, allowing parishioners to be buried near their place of worship. The cemetery is believed to have roughly 570 recorded interments; however,

Tombstones at Posey Chapel Cemetery.

it is likely that the plots of several early settlers were moved from near their homes to Posey Chapel once it was established as a cemetery, with many of these transfers going unrecorded. The first official burial was that of George Morrow, who passed away on July 14, 1845. There is no tombstone for George, as construction of the cemetery was just underway at the time of his death and most of the area was covered with felled timber. Therefore, a proper tombstone could not be placed at the site.

Church services and funerals were held in the log building until 1855, when it was replaced with a larger chapel. Sadly, landowner Wightman Goit did not live to see the new church. He was killed after being hit by a falling tree while clearing land. His death occurred on January 7, 1852, and he was later buried in Posey Chapel Cemetery. Some stories state that the new sanctuary was built as a result of a terrible tragedy. It has long been rumored that the reverend at the time locked many of the parishioners inside the log chapel before setting it on fire, killing everyone inside. Following the incident, the reverend reportedly hanged himself from a tree on the cemetery grounds. However, there is no truth to this story. The new chapel was built to accommodate the surging congregation and the growing cemetery. By the mid-1900s, the church was no longer used as a place of worship, likely due to its rural location. However, some families in

Pavilion at Posey Chapel Cemetery.

the area still used the building for reunions and special events. The City of La Porte considered it a historical landmark. Sadly, the story of the Posey Chapel came to a fiery end on January 26, 1972, when arsonists set the old church ablaze, burning it to the ground. The arsonists were later arrested and convicted of the destruction of the old church. In the years since the fire, a small pavilion has been erected at the site to commemorate the existence of the historic Posey Chapel.

The story of the crazed preacher is not the only tale to haunt the grounds of Posey Chapel Cemetery. Many locals and ghost hunters alike have frequented the cemetery, hoping to catch a glimpse of one of the many spectral inhabitants thought to wander the old burial ground. Many witnesses have reported encountering shadow people in the area, along with the apparition of a woman dressed in white. She has been heard singing, accompanied by what many people claim to be acoustic guitar music, leading them to believe that she may be a former parishioner of the chapel. She seems to be rather pleasant and chatty, with many witnesses stating that she has attempted to make contact with them. Some people believe she could be the spirit of Mary Goit, the daughter of Wightman. She passed away in July 1855 at roughly the age of sixteen. Her funeral was the first to be held in the new Posey Chapel. Lights have also been seen bouncing throughout the cemetery, along with the sound of bells, similar to those that oxen would have worn as they roamed the area in the early days of the church.

While most of the activity at Posey Chapel Cemetery seems rather benign, the site does have a few dark tales to share. Reports of a hellhound at the site have the creature running in front of vehicles, causing them to swerve, but when drivers look in their rearview mirror, the canine is gone. A small child has been heard in the cemetery calling for its mama, and phantom baby buggies have been reported to roll down the hill toward the road. The spirit of a little girl has reportedly attempted to make contact with visitors to the area, but some fear she may not be what she seems. The pavilion and the woods nearby also appear to be hot spots for activity, with many people reporting red eyes peering back at them and unexplained red lights moving back and forth, with no source such as taillights appearing to be present. Though many people have written off the reported activity in the cemetery as nothing more than legend, others recommend that you take a look for yourself and visit the grounds of Posey Chapel.

6

PATTON CEMETERY
(WALKER CEMETERY)

1401 RUMELY STREET, LA PORTE, IN 46350
LA PORTE COUNTY
HOURS: DAILY 6:00 A.M. TO 8:00 P.M.
WEBSITE: HTTPS://WWW.FACEBOOK.COM/PAGES/PINE-LAKE-
CEMETERY/120717681275591

Patton Cemetery is a hauntingly beautiful spot filled with mature hardwood trees that give visitors the feeling of being far removed from the cemetery's residential location. The grounds are quite large and divided into several sections. A map can be found online that serves as a handy tool for those looking to traverse the grounds. The land was commissioned as La Porte's second cemetery in 1841 by John Walker, a founder of the city. Unfortunately, Walker experienced financial trouble and had difficulty overseeing the cemetery. Davidson Patton, who arrived in the area in 1838, was then charged with overseeing the burial ground, thus giving the cemetery its name. The grounds are home to some of the oldest graves in the area, with the first recorded burial at Patton Cemetery being that of Abinade Clarkson Patton, who passed away on February 2, 1844. She was the first wife of Davidson Patton. He would marry on two more occasions. His second union also ended in death when Henrietta "Harriett" Knapp Patton died on November 30, 1860. She is buried in the Plains section of Patton Cemetery, next to Abinade, with both women sharing a tombstone with Davidson. His third wife, Eliza Gregory Patton, also failed to outlive Davidson. Her death occurred on July 21, 1888. She, too, is buried in the

Plains section, not far from the graves of Davidson and his first two wives. Following Eliza's death, Davidson lived for roughly another year and a half before finally joining his wives in his namesake cemetery on January 26, 1890, at the age of seventy-seven.

Patton Cemetery is one of two large burial grounds in La Porte, serving as a sister cemetery of sorts with the nearby Pine Lake Cemetery due to their association with the victims of "black widow" Brynhild Paulsdatter Størseth, more commonly known as Belle Gunness. Patton Cemetery is the final resting place of three of her victims. Belle came to America in 1881, first living in Chicago and marrying department store night watchman Mads Ditlev Anton Sorenson in 1884. They opened a candy shop, but that endeavor proved to be unsuccessful. It wasn't long before a series of unfortunate events began to unravel in Mads and Belle's life. Their two oldest children, Axel and Caroline, died while still infants from acute colitis, with many believing that Belle poisoned them due to the similarities in symptoms. Belle and Mads received insurance proceeds for the loss of both of the children. They went on to have two more daughters: Myrtle in 1897, followed by Lucy in 1898. The family's happiness was short-lived, though, as they lost both their store and home in two separate fires, collecting insurance money in both cases. Not long after, Mads suffered massive heart failure and passed away on July 30, 1900, at forty-six years of age. His family was immediately suspicious of Belle, but their concerns were quickly dismissed by authorities. Mads is buried in Forest Home Cemetery in Forest Park, Illinois, along with his two infant children.

Following the sudden loss of her husband, Belle traveled with her two remaining daughters to La Porte. After arriving, it wasn't long before she had set her sights on a new husband, widower Peter Gunness, who had already lost an infant daughter prior to meeting Belle. The couple married on April 1, 1902, and blended Belle's family of three with Peter and his daughters, Swanhild and Jennie Gunness. However, tragedy struck a mere seven days following their union with the sudden death of Peter's youngest daughter, Jennie, who was only seven months old. Records do not indicate where the child was buried. As with Belle's previous marriage, it wasn't long before tragedy struck once again with the death of Peter Gunness on December 16, 1902. Belle reported that he died in a freak accident involving the auger of a sausage grinder falling from a shelf and striking Peter on the head, killing him instantly. He was buried in Patton Cemetery in the tier section, tier two, grave three. His original monument was replaced with a modern tombstone in the years following his death.

Grave of Peter Gunness at Patton Cemetery. He was a victim and husband of Belle Gunness.

It soon became apparent to Belle that marrying men was taking too much time and slowing her flow of funds, so she turned back to one of the means she used to meet men while living in Chicago: the "Lonely Hearts" columns printed in newspapers and catering to the Scandinavian population of the United States. She met a variety of suitors this way, inviting several to come stay at her farm. These gentlemen included John Moo, Henry Gurholdt, Olaf Svenherud, Ole B. Budsburg and Olaf Lindbloom, all of whom traveled to La Porte with the intention of wooing Belle, only to have their money drained and then to never be heard from again. It was also during this time that Belle gave birth to a son, Philip Gunness, in 1904. Records do not indicate who may have fathered this child. Belle also adopted young Jennie Olsen. Jennie's mother had passed away, and her father, not knowing how to care for a young child, believed that Belle would tend to Jennie's needs better than he could.

Belle's last suitor at the farm was Andrew Helgelien. He and Belle had corresponded for several months when Andrew finally made the decision to take the $3,000 that he had to his name and head to La Porte. Andrew left his home in South Dakota in January 1908 to answer Belle's ad with the intention of marrying the widow. His family in South Dakota waited to hear of Andrew's arrival in Indiana, but they received no word from him. His brother Asle sensed that something was amiss and sent a letter to Belle inquiring as to the whereabouts of his brother. Belle responded cordially, stating that Andrew had arrived at the farm but that their match was not meant to be and that she believed Andrew had left Indiana for Norway with the intention of visiting family. Something about her story did not sit right with Asle, so he immediately found himself traveling from South Dakota to Indiana, navigating the same route his brother had taken months before. Asle's plan was to question Belle personally about the fate of his brother. Belle, too, sensed that her ruse had run its course. By the time Asle arrived in April 1908, Belle's farmhouse lay in smoking ruins and investigators were already on the scene removing bodies from the farmhouse. They discovered the charred corpses of three children, along with that of a headless woman lying not far from Belle's surprisingly intact dentures. The coroner identified the children as Myrtle, Lucy and Philip, the biological offspring of Belle Gunness. Before the fire, Belle informed many in the city that she had concerns that one of her farmhands, Ray Lamphere, may have been infatuated with her. She feared that he could do harm to her and her children, as she had repeatedly ignored his advances. Police may have initially believed that Lamphere was the sole culprit of the fire, but after searching the property, particularly the area of Belle's chicken yard, where the remains of no fewer than ten bodies were found, the investigators were convinced that Belle had been the mastermind of the fire and that the remains of the headless woman, who was far smaller in stature than Belle, could not possibly be her. The remains of the unidentified woman and Belle's three children tested positive for strychnine and arsenic. Not long after Asle arrived, he was quite shocked to learn that his brother's remains had been found in a fairly fresh shallow grave on Belle's property. An autopsy was ordered and revealed that Andrew had died by the same means as that of the Gunness children. He had large amounts of arsenic and strychnine in his stomach. The body of fifteen-year-old Jennie Olsen was also found buried at the site, with many believing that Belle had murdered her two years earlier, as that was the last time anyone reported seeing the child. When previously asked about Jennie's whereabouts, Belle had claimed she was at a Lutheran school in Los Angeles. The remains of Andrew Helgelien and Jennie Olsen were buried in Patton Cemetery in the tier section, not far from Peter Gunness in tier three. The remains of Belle's three children were interred with the girls' father, Mads, in Illinois. However, this has come into question in recent years, with many believing that the remains in the children's graves could have gotten mixed up with other bodies discovered at the farm and could possibly contain additional previously unknown victims of Belle.

Right: Grave of Andrew Helgelien at Patton Cemetery. He was a victim of Belle Gunness.

Below: Grave of Jennie Olsen at Patton Cemetery. Olsen was a victim and adopted daughter of Belle Gunness.

The tales of Belle Gunness's chicken yard and the many victims found within did not end with the discovery of their remains, as their story will pick up later in La Porte's Pine Lake Cemetery. Ray Lamphere, Belle's former farmhand, was apprehended in May 1908, and when questioned, he admitted to setting the fire at the behest of Belle but outright denied having anything to do with the many bodies discovered on the grounds. He was convicted of arson on November 28, 1908, and sentenced to serve two to fourteen years at the Michigan City prison. He passed away a little over a year following his conviction on December 30, 1909, from complications with the tuberculosis that he had contracted while incarcerated. He was laid to rest in Rossburg Cemetery in La Porte.

As for Belle, it is believed that she killed as few as nineteen men, women and children, with the number more likely closer to forty, as additional potential victims were reported in Illinois, Wisconsin, Ohio, West Virginia, Minnesota and Montana. Belle's grisly legend circulated throughout the United States, with many people referring to her as "Lady Bluebeard" or "Belle the Butcher." But what happened to Belle Gunness after she left La Porte? There were many sightings throughout the years, the last occurring in 1931 in Los Angeles, the same city where Belle had claimed she sent Jennie Olsen for school. A woman named Esther Carlson died while awaiting trial on charges that she had killed her employer. Esther bore a sticking resemblance to Belle and was about the same age. Looking into her background, authorities discovered that two of Esther's husbands and one suitor also died unusual deaths. That information, coupled with the fact that Esther didn't begin appearing in records until 1908—the same year as the fire at Belle's farm—led many to believe that Esther may have been a likely candidate for the alias that Belle used following her escape from La Porte. Esther is interred at San Jacinto Cemetery in San Jacinto, California.

Though Patton Cemetery is most often associated with being the final resting place of three of Belle's victims, it is also reported to have its share of ghostly activity, including reports of shadowy apparitions being seen and disembodied voices heard on the grounds and caught on EVP. Large orbs have been photographed throughout the area; many people say that they are often darker than typical orbs. Visitors share that they get an overwhelming feeling of being watched, and some claim to feel extreme sorrow when near the graves of Belle's three victims. Whether they are experiencing paranormal activity or the power of suggestion due to Belle's notorious history is hard to say. For those interested in finding out more, the cemetery is open until 8:00 p.m., allowing for visitors to wander the cemetery at dusk in the fall and winter months.

7

PINE LAKE CEMETERY

1367 PINE LAKE ROAD, LA PORTE, IN 46350
LA PORTE COUNTY
HOURS: DAWN UNTIL DUSK
WEBSITE: HTTPS://WWW.FACEBOOK.COM/PAGES/PINE-LAKE-
CEMETERY/120717681275591

Pine Lake is La Porte's third cemetery, offering beautiful views of the cemetery's namesake, the nearby Pine Lake. The cemetery was first proposed in August 1856, when the old city cemetery was deemed too full for further interments. The first burial is that of Theodosia Russell Darling, who died at the age of seventy in 1858. She was originally interred at the old city cemetery, but not long after her burial, lots became available in Pine Lake for both new burials and transfers. Theodosia's family purchased a lot for her, and she was moved to Pine Lake.

By 1871, the city cemetery had fallen into such disrepair that local officials decided that all burials should be moved to Pine Lake. As the city cemetery was quite large, a deadline of January 1, 1894, was given to allow time for all inhabitants to be transferred to their new resting places. In all, 723 bodies were exhumed; only 231 had markers allowing for identification. Those with stones were reinterred in individual plots, while the other 492 souls were buried in a mass grave on the grounds of Pine Lake Cemetery. The old stones from the city cemetery were placed in a rectangle to signify that these were the unknown burials from the city cemetery. The transfer of so many bodies also led to strange stories regarding the state of some of those disinterred from the city cemetery. The remains of one woman who was buried in 1841 seemed to have the hallmarks of someone who had been buried alive, as she was found face down in her coffin, her remains appearing to be somewhat twisted. A mother and daughter who had passed away on the same date were found buried in the same grave.

The mass grave at Pine Lake is not the only one of its kind on the grounds. A smaller mass burial plot is marked with a single stone; these are the victims found in the chicken yard of Belle Gunness. She reportedly drugged each of the men before hitting them in the head with a hammer or shovel, likely shattering their skulls. She would then load the body onto a wooden cart, transferring it either to her chicken yard for burial or possibly to her hog pen, allowing for much of the evidence to be consumed before collecting the remaining bones for burial. Many believe there were the remains of roughly ten men on her farm, with the bones being split between two caskets and placed in a lonely section of Pine Lake Cemetery often reserved for paupers' graves. The men spent many years with no marker, until 2008, on the one-hundredth anniversary of Belle's fiery departure from La Porte, when a new headstone was erected to honor the memory of her unidentified victims. Due to the new monument, the grave has become a curiosity of sorts in the cemetery, with locals and tourists alike visiting the site to pay their respects to the men who died by the poison bottle of Belle Gunness. For those interested in learning more about Belle and her many victims, the La Porte County Historical Society offers a ghastly, yet absorbing, exhibit on the life and crimes of Belle Gunness, including the very cart she used in her dastardly deeds.

Pine Lake is also reported to have a bit of strange activity that occurs on the grounds. Mist-like shadows have been seen floating above the tombstones, and many who have taken photographs in the cemetery report multiple orbs appearing in the

Memorial at Pine Lake Cemetery for the unidentified victims of Belle Gunness.

pictures. Those who have experienced this activity seem to indicate that it occurs frequently in the area of the mass grave belonging to the former city cemetery inhabitants as well as near the grave of Belle's victims. Orbs have also been captured throughout the grounds and in high frequency, leading some to believe that this activity is directly related to the unnamed and often ignored deceased residents of Pine Lake Cemetery who may now be making their presence known to the living visitors to the beautiful burial ground by the lake.

PART II

CENTRAL INDIANA

8

FOREST HILL CEMETERY

2181 East County Road 200 North, Greencastle, IN 46135
Putnam County
Hours: April 1–September 1, 8:00 a.m. to 7:30 p.m.;
September 2–March 31, 8:00 a.m. to 5:00 p.m.
Website: https://cityofgreencastle.com/departments/cemetery

Forest Hill is a well-manicured garden cemetery located on 133 acres in the city of Greencastle. It is not far from the city center and quite easy to find. The cemetery was established in 1865 with the burial of John McKee, a former Putnam County sheriff. He had been in Pittsburgh, Pennsylvania, when he fell ill and passed away. His body was returned to Greencastle, and his burial occurred on September 11, 1865. In the years since, the inhabitants of Forest Hill have grown to outnumber the living residents of Greencastle, with more than eleven thousand burials in the cemetery. Forest Hill was added to the National Register of Historic Places on September 14, 2015.

Forest Hill is also home to some very unique mausoleums and monuments, with the cemetery having influences of art deco and Gothic Revival architecture. Two mausoleums in particular are on the lowest ground in the cemetery in what appears to be a large ditch, and it seems they may have experienced a bit of flooding over the years. Another notable monument is that of Dr. John Clark Ridpath. He was an author and educator serving as vice-president of Asbury University, now known

Grave of John McKee at Forest Hill Cemetery.

Right: Grave of Dr. John Clark Ridpath at Forest Hill Cemetery.

Below: Community Abbey at Forest Hill Cemetery.

as DePauw University. He died in New York City on July 31, 1900. His body was returned to Greencastle for burial at Forest Hill. The cemetery also contains a building known as the Forest Hill Abbey, a community mausoleum for the citizens of Greencastle.

Forest Hill is also the final resting place of an unfortunate soul named Pearl Bryan. Her story is a sad one, beginning with an unexpected pregnancy at the age of twenty-three in 1896. Pearl came from an affluent Greencastle family. Her father worked as a farmer, stock breeder and dairy operator. Pearl had become acquainted with a gentleman named Scott Jackson, quickly falling head over heels for her new suitor. Her family was quite pleased with the arrangement, as Jackson was a dental student with a promising career and would certainly be able to provide for Pearl. However, the relationship was not to be. Jackson left Pearl to move to Cincinnati. It wasn't long after that Pearl discovered she was with child. She quickly notified Jackson of the new development and, with his insistence, agreed to have an abortion. He asked that she travel to Cincinnati for the procedure, and Pearl agreed to do so, telling her family that she was traveling to Indianapolis, so as not to alert them that anything was amiss.

Not long after her arrival in Cincinnati, Jackson introduced her to a close friend of his, Alonzo Walling, who was also a dental student. Initially, Jackson and Walling tried a variety of concoctions to cause Pearl to miscarry, but these attempts were unsuccessful. On the evening of Pearl's death, Jackson purchased a large amount of cocaine and was later seen by a bartender at the Wallingford Saloon, spiking Pearl's drink, likely with some of the cocaine he had purchased earlier. The cocaine failed to induce an abortion, much to the chagrin of Jackson, who now apparently felt that he was left with limited options. Jackson and Walling then hired a driver to take them, along with Pearl, to an abandoned slaughterhouse in nearby Wilder, Kentucky. Once there, Jackson and Walling put their new plan into action. Pearl was likely subdued as a result of the cocaine, and the men began using dental tools in an attempt to give Pearl an abortion. They botched this attempt, too, likely causing great physical damage to Pearl, along with blood loss. It is likely that, at this point, the men realized that Pearl was in need of medical attention. Since both were aspiring dentists and likely to face repercussions affecting their futures, Jackson and Walling made the gruesome decision to use the dental tools to decapitate Pearl in an attempt to disguise her identity. It is said that they tossed her head into a well in the slaughterhouse and then disposed of her body in a field at the nearby Locke Farm. However, other accounts state that Jackson returned to Cincinnati with Pearl's head, disposing of it somewhere within the city.

Pearl's headless body was discovered on February 1, 1896. An autopsy was conducted to determine the cause of death. The coroner discovered that Pearl had been roughly five months along at the time of her death and that she had likely been alive during the decapitation due to the large amount of blood, both at the slaughterhouse and in the field. High amounts of cocaine were also present in her system, further confirming the bartender's report that he had seen Jackson slip something into her drink. Prussic acid was also found during the autopsy. This likely would have killed Pearl had the men not opted to take such a grisly step. Following the initial discovery of Pearl's body, locals flocked to the field to get a glimpse of the macabre scene for themselves. Many of them took souvenirs, including bloody leaves. Some people even set up stands to sell the items taken from the site. But the most morbid development was yet to come. Someone had managed to take possession of Pearl's unborn fetus, putting the child in a jar that had once held peppermint sticks and charging a fee for anyone requesting to see it. The baby was never given a proper burial, and records do not state what became of the jar or the child.

Fortunately, Jackson and Walling had left Pearl with one easily identifiable item: her shoes. As Pearl came from a well-to-do family, her shoes were quite expensive and rather easy to track back to a local cobbler in Greencastle. Investigators discovered that only two women had purchased those shoes, one of the buyers being quite alive and the other being Pearl Bryan. Once her identity was known, it wasn't long before Jackson and Walling were arrested in Ohio. However, they were not immediately charged, as authorities were unsure if the murder had occurred in Ohio or Kentucky. The men were later charged in Kentucky, a state with stricter laws regarding the deaths of unborn children. During the trial, letters between Jackson and Walling were introduced into evidence. They detailed Jackson's plan to end Pearl's pregnancy. In the end, both men were found guilty of Pearl's murder and scheduled to be hanged in March 1897. In the days leading up to his execution, Walling continued to claim that he had nothing to do with Pearl's murder, although he did admit to being privy to Jackson's plans. Jackson, on the other hand, was devoid of remorse and refused to speak about the murder or to reveal the location of Pearl's head. On the evening before their executions, Walling and Jackson were given cigars and allowed to socialize with other inmates in the Newport Jail. At one point, Jackson claimed that Walling had not been involved in Pearl's death, likely a last-minute attempt to spare his friend from the gallows. The confession of sorts was sent to the governor, who stated that unless Jackson provided further details about Pearl's death, both executions would move forward as planned. Jackson refused the request, and both men were hanged simultaneously the following day without revealing the location of Pearl's head, which remains a mystery to this day. Jackson's body was quickly cremated to avoid any desecration of his corpse and to prevent souvenir seekers from treating him as they had treated Pearl.

In the years following Pearl's death, the abandoned slaughterhouse was demolished. A new building was erected on the site in the 1920s to house a speakeasy and casino. In the 1950s, the building served as nightclub called the Latin Quarter. In an odd twist of fate, Johanna, the daughter of the Latin Quarter's owner, found herself in a similar situation to that of Pearl. She had fallen in love with a singer named Robert Randall and had become pregnant. She announced her intention to leave town with Randall to start a family. However, her father, who disapproved of the union, used his criminal connections to have Robert Randall killed. When Johanna learned of her father's betrayal, she poisoned him and took her own life in the basement, not far from the former slaughterhouse well where it is believed that Jackson placed Pearl's head. The former Latin Quarter found new life in 1978 as a honky-tonk nightclub known as Bobby Mackey's Music World. Interestingly, Bobby Mackey's full name is Robert Randall Mackey, adding to the coincidences that seem to abound on the grounds of the former slaughterhouse. The building lays claim to the ghosts of Johanna and Pearl Bryan with the story of Pearl's death changed ever so slightly to state that Jackson and Walling may have been involved with satanic activity and that this is what led them to murder Pearl. For those interested in learning more about Johanna, Pearl and the paranormal activity at Bobby Mackey's, ghost tours and investigations are offered throughout the year. However, Bobby Mackey's isn't the only location to claim the ghost of Pearl Bryan.

Visitors to Forest Hill have long reported that Pearl's spirit may actually remain in the cemetery, with many stories stating that a female apparition has been encountered near the Bryan family plot. Many reports describe the spirit as being headless and wandering rather aimlessly among the tombstones, as if she is looking for something, perhaps her lost head or the child who never received a proper burial. However, other stories state that a similar female apparition has been seen in the cemetery, but her body is intact and she clearly has her head. Could this be Pearl or another resident of Forest Hill? Orbs have also been photographed throughout the cemetery,

Bryan family plot at Forest Hill Cemetery. It is the final resting place of Pearl Bryan.

particularly in and around the Bryan family plot, as it seems to be the most paranormally active location on the grounds. Sadly, in the years since Pearl's death, her tombstone, much like the site where her body was found, has been frequented by souvenir hunters intent on not letting her rest peacefully. They have picked away at the tombstone, leaving nothing more than the base. Visitors leave pennies, heads-up, for Pearl so that she won't be headless after all. For those wishing to visit Pearl, the GPS coordinates to her grave site are available via Find A Grave, or one can drive through the cemetery and look for the Bryan family plot. Pearl's grave is close to the road and easily recognizable due to the damage it has sustained. Please be respectful when visiting the cemetery and be sure to leave a penny, heads-up, for Pearl.

9

BOONE-HUTCHESON CEMETERY

SOUTH COUNTY ROAD 450 NORTH, REELSVILLE, IN 46135
PUTNAM COUNTY
HOURS: OPEN TWENTY-FOUR HOURS
WEBSITE: HTTP://WWW.PCFOUNDATION.ORG/BOONEHUTCHESONCEMETERY.HTM

Boone-Hutcheson Cemetery, often shortened to Boone-Hutch by locals, sits atop a rolling hill, offering magnificent views of the rural countryside as well as the nearby Houck covered bridge and Big Walnut Creek. The grounds are in pristine condition, though many of the tombstones have become illegible over time and some markers have fallen over. A few have been repaired using metal bars and, in one instance, duct tape. The cemetery dates to 1812, with the earliest recorded interment being in 1818, of a child belonging to the Sellers family whose tombstone would have read "Infant" Sellers. However, it would seem that this tombstone no longer remains, or if it does, it is one of the many memorials that can no longer be read. Boone-Hutch served as a burial ground for the first settlers to the area, including the Hutchesons, Risslers and some descendants of famed frontiersman Daniel Boone. According to records, the cemetery has roughly one thousand burials, twenty-one of those belonging to the Boone family and eighty-four being members of the Hutcheson family. The land was originally the dividing line between the properties of Squire Boone and Randolph Hutcheson; the men likely chose the site for a burial ground due to the difficulty in using it for farming and the beauty and convenience of the location. Randolph Hutcheson lived on

Boone-Hutcheson Cemetery sign.

the land with his wife, Mary Elizabeth Warner Hutcheson, and they raised twelve children there, with one child passing away at a young age. Both Randolph and Mary lived into their seventies, and they are buried on the grounds of Boone-Hutch, along with six of their children.

Throughout the years, there has been some confusion regarding the Boones buried in Boone-Hutch. Many people believe that the sister of Daniel Boone and Squire Boone Jr. is buried there, along with some of Squire's children. In actuality, the Boones buried in the cemetery are the children and grandchildren of Moses Boone, the nephew of Daniel and Squire Boone Jr. Moses is one of the many Boones buried in Boone-Hutch. In life, he had fourteen children; two of the boys, Daniel and Squire, were named in honor of Moses's famous uncles. Daniel passed away on October 20, 1887, choosing to be buried in Boone-Hutch not far from his older sister, Susannah "Susan" Boone Rissler, who died on November 19, 1885. Squire and his second wife, Phebe Rissler Boone—coincidently, the sister of Susan's husband, William Rissler—lived in Indiana for a time before moving to Iowa. Sadly, they lost three children during their time here. Melmoth (one year old), Matilda (seven) and Irv (eleven) all died within a span of eight years, and all were buried in Boone-Hutch Cemetery. Phebe's death causes a bit of confusion as well. During a trip

Grave of Susan Boone Rissler at Boone-Hutch Cemetery.

to Boone-Hutch, one may notice that Phebe Boone is mentioned on a memorial stone noting Susan's death and commemorating the deaths of Squire and Phebe's children. The wording of this monument makes it seem as if Phebe is buried in the cemetery as well. But you could spend all day wandering Boone-Hutch and never find a tombstone for her; she is buried next to Squire in the Squire Boone Cemetery in Luther, Iowa. It is likely that she and Squire, along with the family members they left behind, have been memorialized on this stone so that future generations will remember the legacy of the Boones in Putnam County.

Boone-Hutch is also known to locals for another reason. Many visitors to the site have reported paranormal activity throughout the cemetery and in a small patch of woods nearby. The most commonly circulated tale is that of a policeman dressed in a 1950s-style uniform. He is often spotted near the entrance to the cemetery and has also been seen holding a blue light. He rarely interacts with visitors, instead preferring to watch their movements on the grounds before finally disappearing. However, if someone enters the cemetery with the intention to do damage to the site, the policeman will chase them back to their car. It seems that the police officer is a spectral caretaker of sorts for the cemetery. His blue light has been seen moving among the tombstones, almost as if he is making his nightly rounds to ensure

Grave of Matilda and Irv Rissler at Boone-Hutch Cemetery.

Grave of George McIntosh at Boone-Hutch Cemetery. This is one of many older, intact tombstones.

that all is well at Boone-Hutch. Other reports claim that a strange car has followed them to the entrance of the cemetery, but before the vehicle can turn in behind them, it disappears, with some people stating that they were sure it was an older model police cruiser.

The cemetery is home to a number of other apparitions, including that of a teenage boy. He has communicated through EVP on a few occasions and by all accounts is a friendly ghost. He has been known to favor some of the nightly visitors to the cemetery, with some accounts even stating that he has occasionally followed folks home. He doesn't seem to stay long but playfully makes his presence known before returning to Boone-Hutch a short time later, likely waiting for his next escapade. The spirit of a woman has been encountered in the cemetery as well. Many people say she is a demonic entity and should not be approached. A whispered voice is sometimes heard; many witnesses state that it sounds female. Other visitors have also reported an ominous feeling and the sensation that they are being watched.

The most frightening tales of Boone-Hutch involve a cave located in the small wooded area to the west of the cemetery. This cave is on private property, so you are trespassing if you venture over the fence and into the trees. Needless to say, many people have disregarded this warning and found themselves wishing they hadn't. Legend states that there is a grave next to the entrance to the cave and that upon entering one will see very old and dilapidated caskets hanging overhead. Other, more horrifying tales state that the ghostly bodies of the coffins' inhabitants have been known to fall from their funerary boxes, landing on the ground in front of shocked onlookers before disappearing in front of their eyes. This area is also thought to be home to the hellhounds of Boone-Hutch. Their glowing red eyes are often seen moving about in the trees not far from the entrance to the cave. These hellhounds will often venture into the cemetery. Those who have encountered them claim to have heard deep growls or that they witnessed a large black dog with red eyes lunge at or chase their vehicles. Because Boone-Hutch is open twenty-four hours, this is one cemetery that should definitely be visited after dark. Though the grounds often appear tranquil, always remember that looks can be deceiving, even in the most hauntingly beautiful of locations.

10

CARPENTER CEMETERY
(ONE HUNDRED STEPS CEMETERY
OR CLOVERLAND CEMETERY)

7114–7140 NORTH COUNTY ROAD 675 WEST, CLOVERLAND, IN 47834
CLAY COUNTY
HOURS: DAWN UNTIL DUSK

Carpenter Cemetery, or One Hundred Steps, as it is more commonly referred to, sits atop a hill overlooking a sharp curve and could easily be missed were it not for the imposing set of stairs leading to it. The location began as a rural family cemetery and was created by the Carpenter family. The first recorded burial was that of George Carpenter III, who passed away at the age of sixty-eight on December 17, 1872. He and his wife, Elizabeth, had moved from Pennsylvania to present-day Cloverland in 1828. The couple had eleven children; three daughters and one son are also buried in the family cemetery. There may be older burials on the grounds, some possibly dating to the 1860s, but there is no record of any burials prior to George's death.

For years, the original staircase included one hundred steps, giving the cemetery its unique moniker. But over time, the stairs became broken and cracked, many of them disappearing into the hillside. The steps have since been replaced with a brand-new staircase. But one thing remains the same: there are still one hundred steps. A chain-link fence has also been added in recent years in an attempt to protect the highly vandalized location. It is thought that there are roughly 350 to 400 burials in the cemetery. Sadly, due to human intervention, many of the tombstones have been pushed over or destroyed entirely; many of the earlier memorials are marked with nothing more than a sunken spot in the ground. The location has longed served as a hangout for local teenagers and ne'er-do-wells, some of whom have had ill intent toward the old cemetery. The first desecration of the burial ground occurred in 1892. You see, in the days of early medicine, it could be difficult for medical schools to acquire cadavers for their students, leading to a rise in the prosperous profession of grave robbing. With One Hundred Steps being located one county over from Asbury College, now DePauw, the cemetery was likely visited by "Resurrectionists" on more than one occasion, as was the case on November 19, 1892. Two years prior, Emma West, the daughter of local farmer George West, had passed away after falling victim to one of the known infectious diseases of the time. Emma was buried at One Hundred Steps in an individual plot. Her father later purchased a family plot in the cemetery and intended to have Emma interred there. However, when the time came to transfer Emma to the new plot, the workers were shocked to discover that Emma's coffin was upside down and that her remains were missing. No one was ever arrested for the crime, and George West moved the family plot to another cemetery. Emma's case is the only confirmed incident of grave robbing at One Hundred Steps, but one can't help but wonder if the cemetery was visited on other occasions by "Graveyard Ghouls" looking to steal a corpse.

The stories of One Hundred Steps do not end with the gruesome tale of Emma West. The cemetery is also home to one of the state's well-known urban legends and possibly a bit of ghostly activity as well. Tales have long circulated of locals visiting the cemetery on a moonless night. It is believed that if you climb the stairs, counting all one hundred as you go, at the stroke of midnight, the cemetery's ghostly undertaker will greet you at the top of the hill. He remains silent, serving only as a messenger to reveal the death of the unfortunate soul who encounters him. Legend states that following the vision, the person must immediately descend the steps, counting them once again until they reach one hundred. If they count anything less, they will surely die in the manner revealed by the undertaker's prophecy. In an attempt to avoid learning their potential fate, some visitors have tried to bypass the stairs, instead venturing up the hillside. Most are stopped by an unseen force reported to feel like a hand pushing them to the ground. On further examination, the visitors are often found to have a red mark, sometimes in the shape of a hand, where they were touched. This is referred to as the "Mark of the Devil" by those who have attempted to outwit the undertaker.

Right: The infamous steps at Carpenter/One Hundred Steps Cemetery.

Below: Tombstones at One Hundred Steps.

Though this myth may seem a farfetched, there have been reports of otherworldly occurrences at One Hundred Steps throughout the years. Orbs have been photographed floating above the tombstones and in the woods surrounding the cemetery. Visitors have often reported the feeling of being watched as they wander the grounds. Others have stated that they felt a light touch or tap but when they turned to see who was behind them, no one was there. Teenagers have also reported hearing strange sounds in the cemetery that have sent them fleeing down the hill. Interestingly, some versions of the undertaker story refer to him as the caretaker of the cemetery. With so much vandalism at the location, and at least one instance of grave robbing, it is reassuring to think that the spirit of an old caretaker might remain to watch over the grounds and scare off anyone who plans to do harm to One Hundred Steps.

11
HIGHLAND LAWN CEMETERY

4420 WABASH AVENUE, TERRE HAUTE, IN 47803
VIGO COUNTY
HOURS: DAWN UNTIL DUSK
WEBSITE: HTTPS://TERREHAUTE.IN.GOV/DEPARTMENTS/CEMETERY/HIGHLAND-
LAWN-CEMETERY-1

Highland Lawn Cemetery is the second-largest cemetery in Indiana. It is located on a rolling hill in eastern Vigo County. The plot of land was originally chosen because of its beauty, but also because it was known as a quiet spot, near the outskirts of the growing city of Terre Haute. Initially, there was some concern that the land might be unfit for a burial ground and that it was too wet and marshy, possibly resulting in issues with burials. The land had previously been a farm and also served as an early distillery. Despite concerns, the cemetery opened its gates in 1884. The entrance includes a Romanesque Revival bell tower constructed out of Bedford, Indiana limestone. The Gothic-style arch that greets visitors on arriving at Highland Lawn was designed by Paul Leizt of Chicago and constructed by Edward Hazledine. The cemetery's chapel, built nine years after the cemetery opened, is also of the Romanesque style. It is located on the highest hill in the cemetery. The chapel features gabled roofs, a domed brick basement and stained-glass windows. The first burial at Highland Lawn was that of Samantha McPherson, who died at age thirty on October 13, 1884, of typhoid fever. She was buried in section two, lot six, on October 29, 1884.

Entrance to Highland Lawn Cemetery.

Highland Lawn is home to some very ornate and stunning tombstones, mausoleums and sculptures. The cemetery was added to the National Register of Historic Places on November 29, 1990.

The cemetery is also the final resting place of some of Terre Haute's most notable residents. Eugene V. Debs, a well-known union leader, socialist and activist, is buried in Highland Lawn. Debs ran for president on several occasions and was a constant fixture in Terre Haute in his final years. He died of heart failure at the age of seventy on October 20, 1926. People have been known to travel from all over the United States to visit Debs's small monument in section three. Hollywood vamp and vaudeville actress Valeska Suratt is buried in section 14, lot 475.5. Suratt starred in several successful silent movies before returning to vaudeville, performing well into the 1920s.

Max Ehrmann was a well-known Terre Haute attorney and writer of the poem "Desiderata," which was used on posters and leaflets during the counterculture movement of the 1960s. Ehrmann gained fame when his wife published many of his poems, including "Desiderata," posthumously. His family also once maintained a garment business at the corner of Ninth and Wabash, with Max running his law practice from the location, though many said he tended to very little legal work, instead choosing to focus his time on his writing. The Ehrmann monument is one of many eye-catching

Chapel at Highland Lawn Cemetery.

and beautiful monuments in the cemetery. His grave is adorned with a large sculpture of an angel standing in front of a cross.

Aside from Highland Lawn's many famous residents, the cemetery is also reported to be the home of many spectral inhabitants, as well as a founding member of the spiritualist movement. In May 1867, the First Spiritual Society of Terre Haute was created by Dr. Allen Pence, a local doctor and botanic druggist as well as a promoter and leader of the society. In September 1867, Dr. Pence donated the second floor of his building, Pence Hall, formerly at the southwest corner of Second and Ohio Streets, to be the society's headquarters. Terre Haute soon became known as a spiritualism center, with people coming from all across the United States to attend lectures and séances at Pence Hall. By 1897, spiritualism had more than eight million followers in the United States and Europe. However, numbers quickly declined due to the constant attacks of skeptics, including Harry Houdini. Houdini spent a great deal of his time debunking the methods of famous mediums and attempted to out many of them as frauds, even going so far as to perform their tricks during his stage shows. Spiritualism also hadn't been a very organized movement, mostly because there was infighting and issues among its leaders. Lastly, with so many mediums being denounced as frauds, it became difficult for the public to trust the abilities of those who claimed to be mediums and even more difficult for true mediums to risk exposing themselves to a public that no longer believed their abilities to be valid. As for what became of Dr. Allen Pence, he remained a believer in the "harmonial philosophy" until his death on January 22, 1908. He is buried at Highland Lawn Cemetery in section three. Though no ghostly activity has been reported near Dr. Pence's grave, perhaps he is just waiting for someone to contact him on the other side.

The remains of Claude Herbert are interred in a mausoleum located just off of the main driveway as you head into the cemetery. He is the hero of one of Terre Haute's most tragic stories. On the evening of December 19, 1898, on the northeast corner of Wabash Avenue and Fifth Street in downtown Terre Haute, Claude Herbert was playing Santa Claus at the Havens and Geddes Department Store. At the time, the store took up the entire block and was the largest in Indiana. Claude had been hired two days earlier, having just arrived home from duty during the Spanish-American War. He was in dire need of a job to support his newly widowed mother, Mattie, so he took the position as Santa.

As Claude entertained children in the basement, an incandescent light bulb popped in a display window, setting the items around it on fire. With the fire spreading quickly, another employee notified Claude of the situation. At the time, he was surrounded by nearly thirty young children and was no doubt concerned for their well-being. Despite the dire situation, Claude kept a cool head, opting to stay in character as Santa to calm the children as he shuffled them outside to safety. Upon exiting the building, Claude was alerted to the fact that there could still be victims trapped in the inferno. Rather than allow the responding firefighters to clear the

Allen Pence grave at Highland Lawn Cemetery.

building, Claude's military training went into effect. He threw his Santa costume to the ground and reentered the building. Onlookers last saw him take a deep breath before he disappeared into the thick smoke once again.

As Claude was a newly hired employee, he was unfamiliar with the layout of the large department store and was unaware of a tunnel that led from the basement to a warehouse on Cherry Street. The employees Claude so desperately searched for had escaped through that underground exit. Claude, likely disoriented by the smoke, was unable to find the same exit. Witnesses claim that Claude was last seen trying to save himself from the fire. Some said he jumped from a second-floor window, but others reported seeing him jump from the fifth floor. This seems to be the mostly likely scenario, as that is where he had dressed to play Santa earlier in the evening, and he would have been familiar with that location. Claude Herbert was not the only hero to lose his life that day. Firefighter John Osterloo died, and Henry Nehf, a volunteer firefighter, also perished in a nearby building. The final victim of the fire was store clerk Katie Maloney. She was trapped by the blaze and jumped from a second-story ledge. She hit her head on impact and sustained fatal injuries. Three days later, amid the smoldering ruins of the Havens and Geddes Department Store, estimated to have suffered nearly $2 million in property damage, searchers found two of Herbert's bones. The location led investigators to believe that Claude must have been on the fifth floor when he jumped. Sadly, no further remains were discovered. Claude Herbert had been entirely cremated by the blaze. His remains are interred at the mausoleum at Highland Lawn Cemetery. In the years since Claude's heroic self-sacrifice, strange activity has been reported near the tomb. Visitors who have taken photographs of the area report catching orbs in some of their photographs, with the balls of light centered directly around the Herbert family plot. Whether this is the spirit of Claude Herbert or perhaps a trick of light, it is nice to think that the spirit of Terre Haute's hero may still be looking out for the citizens of the city.

Not far from the Herbert mausoleum is a trio of red tombstones in section 14, lot 198, that reveal the story of a ghastly triple homicide that occurred near West Terre Haute on May 4, 1914. At that time, roughly thirty Romani had traveled from Kentucky to Terre Haute, arriving on May 1, 1914. They parked their wagons near Paris Road and set up a camp. On the day before the homicides, the members of the caravan were in high spirits, as they were in the middle of a raucous celebration, consuming eight kegs of beer, wine and ale in the process. The celebration lasted into the wee morning hours, following which most of the Romani either went to sleep or had passed out from the alcohol consumed throughout the night. But one man remained awake.

John Demetro was a Brazilian Romani tribal chief traveling with the caravan. On the morning of May 4, John remained awake and was probably quite inebriated by that point. He was troubled by rumors circulating throughout the encampment that his common-law wife, Socca Riska, was having an affair. He also believed that Socca's father, Bob, and brother Joe were keeping her secret. At some point, John entered the tent where his family slept. He brutally bludgeoned and shot Socca before turning the gun on his in-laws. The Romani in the camp, alarmed by the gunfire, ran to the Riska tent. They found that Socca and Bob had died instantly from their injuries, but Joe, who had been shot in the face, was still alive, despite the fact that he was missing a large portion of his head. John Demetro, however, could not be found. Some of the Romani rushed to a nearby saloon, while others headed to a local farmhouse to alert the authorities of the murders. The West Terre Haute police arrived quickly and were no doubt shocked by the scene before them. Joe Riska was rushed to a local hospital, but sadly, due to the severity of his injuries, he died the following day. The Romani warned police that Demetro would likely be accompanied by his sixteen-shot Remington rifle. The police, prepared for a shootout with Demetro, found him sitting near his tent, his rifle across his lap. The man stared blankly at the ground, likely already haunted by the murders he had committed. Demetro did not resist arrest but, instead, calmly passed his rifle to police before he was taken into custody without incident.

Following the murders, the caravan moved east of Terre Haute and began preparations for the Riska funeral. The Romani purchased extravagant caskets for the family. They also visited the upscale shops of Terre Haute, purchasing the finest attire for the Riskas. When the day of the funeral came, mourning Romani from throughout the Midwest were in attendance. Incense balls were burned during the graveside service, with pipes and tobacco placed next to each of the bodies. Following the lowering of the coffins, the mourners sprinkled them with soil. Bottles of wine were broken, with the wine being poured atop the coffins in the shape of a cross. According to witnesses at the time, the funeral was quite a sight to behold.

Demetro was arraigned on May 8, 1914. He argued that he was acting in self-defense, but evidence suggested otherwise. He was charged with murder, with a trial to commence in September 1914. The trial would be postponed on two occasions and was later scheduled to begin in September 1915. The trial was attended by many of the Romani who had been present at the camp

Riska graves at Highland Lawn Cemetery.

when the Riska murders occurred. By the end of the day, though, they would find themselves very disappointed with the outcome of the trial. Demetro's defense argued that he could not receive a fair trial in Terre Haute due to the attention that had been given to the case. The judge agreed, and it was decided that the trial would be moved to Rockville, Indiana. Following the change of venue and one more continuance, the prosecutor and Demetro's defense attorney negotiated a plea agreement. The charges for the deaths of Bob Riska and his son were dropped, with Demetro agreeing to plead guilty to second-degree murder for the death of Socca. He was sentenced to life and ordered to serve his time at the Indiana State Prison in Michigan City. In the almost two years since the murders, Demetro had become a shell of his former self. He had lost a considerable amount of weight, and his incarceration had taken a toll on his mental health. He spent the majority of his time in the infirmary while in prison, costing the facility a pretty penny in medical care. Interestingly, after only eighteen months in prison, Demetro was paroled, likely due to his deteriorating health and the estimated cost of his continued care. He was deported to Brazil, where he later died.

Though the murders took place 106 years ago, the Romani community still mourns the loss of the Riska family. In the years since, descendants of the caravan have been seen visiting the graves in Highland Lawn Cemetery. Perhaps they are performing rituals to honor the dead or to ensure that the spirits of the Riska family remain peacefully at rest. However, despite the rituals, otherworldly occurrences have been reported to take place in the area around the Riska graves.

Rumors have circulated about Romani ghosts walking among the tombstones. Could these be the spirits of the Riska family eternally drawn to the site of their burials? Or perhaps they are looking for the caravan they lost so long ago. Orbs have been seen floating above the family plot, usually in multiples, leading some to believe that these could be manifestations of the Riska family. Visitors to the graves have also noted feeling an extreme sense of sadness and grief. The rituals performed by the Romani could account for some of the melancholy felt at the site, almost as if their sorrow has left a permanent mark in the area surrounding the Riska plot. While it is possible that these strange occurrences stem from the Romani belief in the supernatural world, it is also possible that the Riska family is unable to rest following such sudden and violent deaths. Regardless, the trio of graves remains one of the most visited locations in the cemetery.

The story of one mausoleum at Highland Lawn has become an urban legend of sorts among locals, with many referring to it as "a ghostly call from the grave." Martin Alonzo Sheets was a local Terre Haute stockbroker who later retired and became a successful cattle farmer. Like many others in the early twentieth century, one thing concerned Mr. Sheets greatly. He was petrified of being buried alive, also called taphophobia. Being that he had amassed quite a bit of wealth, he came up with a modern plan to address his concerns regarding premature burial. First, he would have a coffin specially designed with inner latches for escape from the inside. Second, he would have a mausoleum built so as to avoid being trapped underground. Lastly and most importantly, he had a phone installed within the mausoleum so that, in the event that he woke up inside his coffin, he would be able to call for assistance. It has been said by many that Sheets had the phone connected directly to the cemetery office so that, in the event of his call, they would need to run mere yards from the office to his mausoleum. Martin Sheets passed away in February 1926. At his request, his body was not embalmed. Sheets was concerned that, should he slip into a coma, the act of embalming or an autopsy would certainly kill him. His mausoleum phone remained connected for a time following Sheets's death at the age of seventy-nine, but no calls were ever placed to the cemetery office and the phone line was eventually disconnected.

Sheets's wife, Susan, would live another three years following her husband's death in 1926. She had been injured in an auto accident in the spring of 1929 and had been living at a home in Paris, Illinois. By all accounts, she had done fairly well following Martin's death, but this is where an otherwise odd story about the fear of premature death takes a more unusual turn. On the day of Mrs. Sheets's death on May 3, 1929, she was found to be tightly clutching the telephone receiver in her hand. The family assumed she died while attempting to contact paramedics for assistance. Following a medical exam, it was discovered that Susan Sheets had died of a massive heart attack. Doctors assumed that the stress of the car accident may have taken a toll of her heart. Plans were made to have Susan interred in the mausoleum along with her husband. Cemetery workers were dispatched to ready the location. Upon entering the mausoleum, one thing was readily obvious to the workers: the phone that had been silent for three long years was now off the hook, as if Martin Sheets had made one last ghostly call to his wife, ushering her to join him on the other side.

This brings me to the most well-known haunt of Highland Lawn, a little bulldog named Stiffy Green. As most locals know, Stiffy Green was the pet bulldog and beloved companion of local florist John G. Heinl. The dog is

Sheets mausoleum at Highland Lawn Cemetery.

described as having a stiff gait and beautiful emerald green eyes, hence the name Stiffy Green. John Heinl originally arrived in Terre Haute in 1863, quickly establishing a thriving floral business. He also met his future wife, Mary Debs, the older sister of Eugene V. Debs, and together they had two sons, Fred and Robert. When he wasn't supplying flowers to the community of Terre Haute, Heinl spent his time working with local organizations and businesses such as the Rose Dispensary and the Rose Orphans Home. He was known to be quite a charitable gentleman and was well liked by the citizens of Terre Haute. Despite Heinl's very busy schedule, he was always accompanied by his bulldog. Stiffy Green is reported to have been a constant sight at Heinl's floral shop at 129 South Seventh Street. Some reports claim that the dog was not very friendly, preferring to spend his time at John's side, though he did take to the occasional customer. Heinl died at his residence on December 30, 1920, at the age of seventy-six.

Following the funeral, his body was taken to his mausoleum in Highland Lawn Cemetery. We have all heard stories about the sadness that a pet can experience on losing their owner, and little Stiffy Green was no different. He would travel daily to the mausoleum, only to be found later by the Heinl family, mournfully waiting on the mausoleum steps for his master to greet him. Finally, the family decided to let Stiffy Green reside at the cemetery full-time, with cemetery staff tending to his needs and ensuring that he had food and a roof over his head. This continued for some time until the day came when the cemetery staff contacted the family to notify them that Stiffy Green had passed away on the mausoleum steps, surely of a broken heart. Of course, it only seemed fitting to have the little bulldog stuffed, compete with a set of emerald glass eyes so that he could spend eternity with the master he was so devoted to in life. Stiffy Green was placed in the back of the mausoleum, to be viewed through the ornate mausoleum door. It wasn't long before stories began to circulate that if you went to Highland Lawn Cemetery at night, you would hear the voice of a man and his small dog, roaming the cemetery, sometimes seen but often only heard in the distance.

But the story doesn't end there. Stiffy Green resided in the mausoleum with his master for several years, and it became a favorite spot for local teenagers, who would go there to shine flashlights into the mausoleum and hope to be greeted by the specters of John G. Heinl and his little green-eyed bulldog. But sometime in the 1980s, vandals entered the cemetery with ill intent toward the little bulldog and, sadly, shot a gun into the Heinl mausoleum, shattering one of Stiffy Green's emerald eyes. Concern grew. In 1989, it was decided that Stiffy Green should be moved to the Vigo

Heinl mausoleum at Highland Lawn Cemetery.

County Historical Society, now located at 929 Wabash Avenue in Terre Haute. He can be found safely residing there today, guarding a small replica of the Heinl mausoleum. But is the tale of Stiffy Green really what it appears to be?

Through the years, I have heard multiple accounts stating that the little dog isn't really a dog at all but instead a statue, which is quite apparent to anyone who visits Stiffy Green today. The most well-known story seems to be that Stiffy Green was nothing more than a favorite lawn ornament of John Heinl. After he passed away, the family thought it fitting to place the statue in the mausoleum as a tribute to Heinl. However, there are still many locals who disagree with this claim. My stepfather once told me a different story. During a brief tenure working at a local monument company in the 1970s, a fellow employee told him that Stiffy Green had indeed been the faithful companion of John Heinl. Following Stiffy Green's death, he was stuffed and put in the mausoleum, as the legend has long stated. But, as the story spread throughout the area and interest grew, the little dog was stolen from the Heinl mausoleum. This act prompted the family to replace him with a concrete statue as a placeholder of sorts, the same statue that now resides in the Vigo County Historical Society, complete with the chipped eye sustained in the shooting. Other locals strongly believe that Stiffy Green had been a real dog but that, perhaps, instead of being stuffed and placed in the mausoleum after John Heinl's death, the family placed a concrete statue in honor of the bond that Heinl and Stiffy Green shared in life. It is obvious that there are varying accounts regarding the little dog in the mausoleum. However, many locals will agree on one thing: there may be some truth to the existence of the stiff-legged little bulldog joining his master for eternal evening strolls through Highland Lawn Cemetery.

12

CROWN HILL CEMETERY

700 Thirty-Eighth Street, Indianapolis, IN 46208
Marion County
Hours: Monday–Saturday, 8:30 a.m. to 5:00 p.m.; closed on Sunday
Website: www.crownhill.org

Crown Hill is Indiana's largest cemetery, as well as the third-largest nongovernmental burial ground in the United States. It boasts 555 acres of beautifully landscaped grounds, adorned with impressive architecture, including a Gothic chapel built in 1875 and the Waiting Station and entry gate at Thirty-Fourth Street, both built in 1885. Upon entering the cemetery, one cannot help but notice the stunning sculptures and monuments that dot the landscape. Crown Hill is also the home of the "Crown," the highest point in Marion County, giving visitors an impressive view of the Indianapolis skyline. Maps of the cemetery are available at the Waiting Station, and it is highly recommended that you pick one up before venturing farther into the cemetery. Guided tours are also offered throughout the year for those wishing to learn more about the inhabitants of Crown Hill without the concern of finding themselves lost on the vast cemetery grounds.

Crown Hill opened its gates on June 1, 1864. The first burial was that of a young wife and mother, Lucy Ann Seaton. She and her husband, John, a Union captain in the Civil War, were new residents of Indianapolis, having moved there from Kentucky. Sadly, the joy they had hoped to experience in their new city was short-lived, as Lucy contracted tuberculosis, passing away

The Waiting Station and entry gate at Crown Hill Cemetery.

at the age of thirty-three on May 26, 1864. Following her death, John posted the funeral announcement in a local newspaper and requested that residents of the family's new city join him in remembering his wife. Lucy's burial followed on June 2, 1864, in section four, lot twenty-eight. Many people attended the services that day. John would be dealt another blow only four short months later, when the couple's daughter, also named Lucy, passed away. She is buried with her mother in Crown Hill. John left Indianapolis not long after and remarried, having two more children. He is buried in Battle Grove Cemetery in Cynthiana, Kentucky.

Crown Hill is also the final resting place of notable Indiana residents and one rather infamous individual. Perhaps one of the most well-known burials is that of notorious gangster and bank robber John Dillinger, who was shot outside the Biograph Theater in Chicago on July 22, 1934. He was buried four days later on July 26 in section forty-four, lot ninety-four, to much fanfare. Supporters of the "modern-day Robin Hood" were quite angry about his death, and riots nearly broke out at the cemetery. Later, on the evening of his burial, souvenir seekers began arriving to take a piece of Dillinger's tombstone, as well as flowers and mud from the site. This would continue for some time, with marker after marker being replaced. Concern soon arose among Dillinger's family, with the decision being made to cover his casket in reinforced concrete so that future souvenir hunters would not be able to access Dillinger himself. A new flat tombstone was also added to the site. In recent years, there has been some discussion about whether the person in Dillinger's grave is actually John Dillinger, with requests being made by his living relatives to exhume the body. This seems to be due to inconsistencies stemming from Dillinger's autopsy, including eye color, fingerprints, anterior teeth, ears and head shape. There have been two previous requests to exhume the body with dates scheduled in each case, but in both instances, the plans fell through. As of now, there is no date set for the exhumation of John Dillinger. Only time will tell if this will actually be allowed by the cemetery.

Grave of Lucy Ann Seaton. Hers is the first burial at Crown Hill.

As for the many famous law-abiding citizens of Crown Hill, Benjamin Harrison, the twenty-third president of the United States and grandson of former president William Henry Harrison, is buried in section thirteen, lot fifty-seven, along with both of his wives. President Harrison was married to Caroline Lavinia Scott until her death at the age of sixty on October 25, 1892. She served as the First Lady of the United States. The couple's oldest child, Russell Benjamin Harrison, is also buried in the family plot, while his sister, Mary Scott Harrison McKee, is buried near the family in section thirteen, lot fifty-three. When her mother became ill, Mary, known as Mamie by many, took over many of the duties of the First Lady, including hosting gatherings at the White House. After losing reelection in 1892 and the death of Caroline the same year, now former president Harrison began courting and later married Mary Scott Lord in 1896. She was the niece of his deceased wife and nearly twenty-five years his junior. They were married five years before Harrison passed away due to complications from pneumonia. They had one child together, Elizabeth Harrison Walker, who is buried in Locust Valley Cemetery in Locust Valley, New York.

Not far from President Harrison's final resting place, also in lot thirteen, is the mausoleum of Booth Tarkington, a well-known novelist and playwright of the early 1900s. He often illustrated his own works as well

Above: The grave of notorious gangster John Dillinger at Crown Hill Cemetery.

Left: Grave site of President Benjamin Harrison and family at Crown Hill Cemetery.

as the novels of other writers. He passed away at the age of seventy-six on May 19, 1946. Tarkington is joined in Crown Hill by his friend and fellow famous literary mind, the "Hoosier Poet" or "Children's Poet," James Whitcomb Riley. Riley was known for such works as *Little Orphant Annie*, *The Raggedy Man* and *Nine Little Goblins*, making him the richest writer of his time. He suffered a stroke in 1911 at the age of sixty-six but never seemed to fully recover, passing away on July 22, 1916. The beloved poet's body laid in state at the Indiana Statehouse rotunda following his death, allowing people to personally pay their respects to Riley. He is buried at the peak of the "Crown" in section sixty-one, lot one, beneath a large Greek Revival monument that includes ten white columns, exquisite landscaping and stairs on either side leading to the sculpture of a small boy reading a book, along with Riley's stone nearby. The monument was built using donations, some of which included pennies from schoolchildren who enjoyed the poems of James Whitcomb Riley. Visitors to the monument often leave coins at the site to be donated to the Riley Hospital for Children, which was established in 1924 and named in honor of Riley. His adult home still stands in the Lockerbie neighborhood of Indianapolis and currently serves as a museum dedicated to his life and work and includes the desk where he sat while writing many of his most famous works.

James Whitcomb Riley is not the only brilliant mind to be laid to rest at Crown Hill. Famed soldier, chemist and founder of Eli Lilly and Company, Colonel Eli Lilly, is interred in an ornate mausoleum in section thirteen, lot nineteen. He attended the Good Samaritan Pharmacy School, training in pharmacology before siding with the Union in the Civil War, serving as a captain and later a colonel of the cavalry. Following his release from service, he tried running a cotton plantation in Mississippi before returning to Illinois to pursue pharmacology. Lilly was dealt a painful blow in 1866 when his young wife, Emily Lemon Lilly, died at the age of twenty-two after contracting malaria. He believed that her death was the result of Indiana's lacking pharmaceutical industry, prompting him to found Eli Lilly and Company in May 1876. His focus was on creating top-of-the line prescription medicines to help the citizens of Indiana and eventually the entire United States. Lilly did find love again, marrying Maria Cynthia Sloane Lilly in 1860. They were married until his death from cancer on June 6, 1898.

In another area of the cemetery is the large monument of inventor Richard Jordan Gatling. His name likely sounds familiar, as he was the founder of the Gatling Gun Company of Indianapolis. His creation consisted of six-gun barrels mounted on a revolving frame powered by

Grave site of the "Hoosier Poet," James Whitcomb Riley, at Crown Hill Cemetery.

Sculpture of a young boy at the grave site of James Whitcomb Riley.

a hand crank that would allow the user to fire multiple shots in rapid succession. The Gatling gun was used during the Civil War, but only for a brief period in 1865. Eventually, with improvements, Gatling's gun could shoot twelve hundred rounds per minute. However, the creation of the smaller, more portable machine gun slowed sales of the Gatling gun, forcing Gatling to merge his company with Colt in 1897. Gatling passed away at the age of eighty-four on February 26, 1903. He was in New York City at the time of his death, so his body had to be returned to Indiana for his interment in section three, lot nine. Eight years following his death, production on the Gatling gun ceased.

Crown Hill is the final resting place of one rather eccentric millionaire, a man who spawned a strange tale that circulated throughout the Indianapolis area for years. Skiles Edward Test was born on October 19, 1889, the child of wealthy parents, Charles Edward Test and Mary Elizabeth Skiles. Following his graduation from high school, Skiles was forced to put off college when his father died, leaving him to take control of the family business. On July 11, 1913, Skiles married his first wife, Josephine Benges. Skiles yearned to invent, so he and Josephine moved to a small house surrounded by acres of farmland where Skiles would have more time to tend to what he loved. He built a small rail system on the property, along with a personal power plant that provided the electricity for his fully functioning farm, which included cows and as many as twenty farmhands. Skiles enjoyed decorating with blue lights at Christmas and often hung bug zappers around the pool, casting a blue glow on the area. By all accounts, despite his eccentricities, Skiles was a generous and well-liked man. He was also quite the animal lover, reportedly keeping 15 St. Bernard dogs and over 150 cats on the property at one time in his later years, even going so far as to have a cat house erected on the grounds where any stray cats that wandered onto the property were allowed to live while enjoying a steady diet of boiled fish, cottage cheese and chicken. Skiles even had a pet cemetery where the cats and dogs were buried in their own caskets, with each having their own tombstone. By all accounts, Skiles and Josephine lived happily on the property. But after twenty years, the couple divorced, and Josephine left for good. This is likely when strange rumors began to spread, particularly among the teenagers of Indianapolis, regarding bizarre activity at the Test farm. Many people claimed that the very much alive Josephine had passed away. Not only that, but the stories also claimed that the bereaved Skiles had taken Josephine's body and placed it in a glass coffin inside

Mausoleum of Eli Lilly at Crown Hill Cemetery.

his residence, adorning the macabre display with bright blue lights, said to be Josephine's favorite color. As the tales burned through the ears of locals, teenagers began venturing out to the farm in an attempt to catch a glimpse of Skiles, or his long-dead partner bathed in blue light. Skiles took the intrusions quite well. During this time, he moved on from Josephine, marrying twice more and even having a child.

By the 1950s, Skiles was finding it difficult to deal with so many interlopers. He was once sued for stealing the clothes and keys of boys who were trespassing on his land and swimming in his pool. In other instances, the St. Bernards were released from their enclosures and fires were lit in farm buildings. Skiles resorted to fencing off the property, but that didn't seem to curb the unwanted visitors. Following his third divorce and the increasing invasions of his home, he began staying with a girlfriend. Skiles passed away on March 18, 1964, at the age of seventy-four. He was buried in the family plot in section twenty-three, lot thirty-four, of Crown Hill Cemetery. His monument is marked by a large stone sundial. Following his death, an auction was held in one of the cow pastures on the property. Thousands of people attended, many just wanting to get a glimpse of the grounds and the casket of Josephine. How disappointed they must have been when they discovered that there was no ghastly shrine to Josephine. The only thing on display that day were Skiles's earthly possessions, all of which were for sale. Following the auction, the house and outbuildings fell into disrepair and were later torn down. Per Skiles's will, the grounds now function as the Skiles Test Nature Park on the northeast side of Indianapolis, just about a twenty-minute drive from his grave at Crown Hill.

Crown Hill is the final resting place of a motley crew of characters and two dogs—Don and Rab, apparently buried there by a board member who broke the rules nearly one hundred years ago. The cemetery is also home to an area shrouded in sorrow and referred to by some as its "dirty little secret." The cemetery has long offered free burial space for poor or orphaned children, with the stipulation that the grave be unmarked. Below Community Hill in section thirty-seven is a mass grave belonging to 699 orphaned children. The grave, measuring roughly thirty feet by fifty feet, contains children who passed away between 1892 and 1980. The children ranged in age from just a few months to fifteen years; just over half of them were boys. All of these children came from three locations within the city of Indianapolis: the Indianapolis Children's Asylum, the Children's Guardian Home and the Asylum for Friendless Colored Children. At one point, there were numbered stones designating the burials of some children, but most

"The Spirit of a Child is Eternally an Angel of Love."
Anonymous

HEARTS REMEMBERED MEMORIAL

CONTRIBUTORS

Care For Kids Foundation

R. Kent Baker	Dan K. Lowring
William T. Brady	Anita Nix
Candy Faulkner	Michael D. Thierwechter
Bill Goetz	Marty Womacks
Greg Krontiris	Barbara Wynne

Children's Guardian Home

Rosie Butler, Director
Paul Browne, Retired

CORPORATE	FOUNDATIONS
Adesa USA	Ayres Foundation
American United Life	Flanner and Buchanan Funeral Center
Bunzl Indianapolis	Eleanor Frenzel Charitable Trust
Clear Channel	W. C. Griffith Trust
CNC System Sales	Guardian Home Foundation
Flanner and Buchanan Funeral Center	Gladys Klest Estate
Guardian Home Guild	Eva Kunkle Estate
Mark-Ritz Corp.	Lilly Endowment
Matthews International Corporation	Ruth Lilly Foundation
Milco Industries	Alice and Kirk McKinney Family Fund
R. Adams Roofing	Randle Family Foundation
Royal Melrose Granite	Stansfield Circle
Sertoma East	Van Riper Family Foundation

INDIVIDUAL	
Wayne Baer	P. E. MacAllister
Robert E. & Bea Baker	Betty & David Moehs
Stephen Blaising	Nancy Ann Morris
Kendall Burdick	Hannah Nichols
Athena Cherpas	John Nohl, M.D.
Jack & Vickie Coombs	Gloria Novotney
Gary & Gina Dankert	Pat O'Connell
Carol Davis	Bill O'Neill
William L. Elder, Jr.	Bill Peddie
Timothy L. Elson	Linda Pence
Brody & Rachel Ertel	Diane Phillips
Carolyn Fuson	Kenneth Rosenfeld
Dan Galligan	Leonard Schutt
Corienne Gettum	John Searight, M.D.
Bill & Marsha Goetz	Anna Sturgeon
Terry & Marcia Goins	Dawn & Norm Tabler
Marvin Graves	Claudia Terry
Tom Hefner	Jane Wildman
Freda Kemp	Turner & Diann Woodard
Jim Kessler	Gary Woods

HEARTS REMEMBERED
"Honoring The Forgotten Children"

The Hearts Remembered Memorial at Crown Hill Cemetery.

were buried without any memorial whatsoever. The earliest deaths were likely a result of typhoid and diphtheria, but many children also fell victim to milk poisoning in a time when formaldehyde was added to milk to kill any pathogenic microorganisms that might be present. Still other children fell prey to neglect and malnutrition. These graves went unnoticed for many years until an intern was asked by the Children's Guardian Home to scour some old files regarding a deed for plots the home owned at Crown Hill. It was during this search that the mass grave was uncovered, shedding light on a dark part of Indianapolis's history. More than one hundred years after the first burial of a child at Community Hill, the Hearts Remembered Memorial was erected on June 4, 2006, to honor the lives of each child buried there. All 699 names were included on the monument. Community Hill also serves as the final resting place of many of the city's widows and indigent citizens, several of them buried beneath tombstones.

With such a dark history, it is no wonder that many ghostly tales have circulated regarding Community Hill, with many of the stories occurring before the mass grave was discovered. Much of the phenomena is said to be heard but not seen. Visitors report the sound of children playing and light humming, though the exact song is never clear. Many believe that the spirits of the children may have bonded together in death, finally having a family in

A unique glimpse at Community Hill through the Hearts Remembered Memorial.

Community Hill at Crown Hill Cemetery.

the afterlife. Many orbs have been photographed at once, floating above the area of the mass grave. A far more concerning report includes the screams of children caught via EVP.

Crown Hill is home to the 1.4-acre National Cemetery that fully encompasses sections nine and ten. It was established in 1866 and is the final resting place of 2,135 soldiers representing every branch of the military. It is in this area that visitors have reported seeing the apparitions of soldiers wandering the cemetery grounds. Some have stated that the spirits appear in uniform and in perfect health, while others report encountering the ghostly apparitions of those injured in battle. Crown Hill is also thought to be the home of a mourning mother. The spectral figure has been spotted in various locations throughout the cemetery. She is always seen walking alone, cradling the body of her young baby. According to some accounts, she appears to be weeping.

The cemetery is also home to a version of the "Resurrection Mary" urban legend. The myth states that on rainy nights, drivers in or near the cemetery on Thirty-Eighth Street have seen an older teenage girl hitchhiking. Many Good Samaritans have stopped to assist the young lady, with the poor girl being soaked from the rain. She requests that they take her to a specific address. Upon arriving, the driver hears no movement in the back seat and, turning around to check on the girl, sees that she has disappeared from the vehicle, leaving only a dry car seat behind. Curious drivers have reportedly knocked on the door of the residence to inquire about the girl, only to be told that she died some years earlier, often in a car accident near the cemetery grounds. With such a long and storied history and so many burials, it is no wonder that Crown Hill has earned a reputation as one of Indiana's haunted cemeteries. If you find yourself curious, take a day to wander the tombstones alone or venture out on one of the nighttime tours. Either way, you might just find yourself face to face with one of the ghostly inhabitants of Crown Hill.

PART III

SOUTHERN INDIANA

13

BRIDGEWATER CEMETERY (OWENS CEMETERY)

COUNTY ROAD 400 SOUTH, SCOTTSBURG, IN 47170
SCOTT COUNTY
HOURS: DAWN UNTIL DUSK
WEBSITE: HTTPS://WWW.FACEBOOK.COM/PAGES/BRIDGEWATER-
CEMETARY/161763370519981

Bridgewater Cemetery sits on a dead-end road, atop a hill, surrounded by farmland on all sides. At one time, the road continued east to State Road Three, but this is no longer the case, causing the cemetery to be quite isolated. This area is also steeped in legend, with stories dating to the early 1800s claiming that this small rural burial ground began as a family homestead. Visitors to the location might be confused to see graves on the outside of the cemetery gates. As the legend goes, the Bridgewater family were slave owners, and sadly, when one of the slaves passed, they were unceremoniously buried outside of the cemetery, beneath an oak tree that some locals refer to as the "Death Tree." The myth further states that the large tree was used for hangings, but no evidence seems to exist to corroborate this story. However, one part of the tale is true. Bridgewater Cemetery is indeed a small rural family cemetery started by the affluent Bridgewaters. The earliest grave was that of Samuel Bridgewater, the son of English duke Immanuel Bridgewater. On traveling to America, Samuel and his two brothers, Elias and Isaac, aligned themselves with George Washington and served during the Revolutionary War. Samuel passed away on May 17, 1827. He shares a tombstone with his wife, Mary Ann Coffman Bridgewater, an accomplished doctor. A modern stone replaced their earlier memorials. Both Samuel and Mary were survivors of the Pigeon Roost massacre, which occurred shortly after the War of 1812 began in September of that year. Pigeon Roost was a settlement near present-day Underwood, Indiana. It was attacked by a band of Native Americans. The settlers in the community killed four of the attackers, but the families of Pigeon Roost lost nine adults and fifteen children that day, with the Native Americans taking two children with them as they fled. Pigeon Roost was rebuilt following the massacre, but many of the citizens, including Samuel and Mary Bridgewater, left with their children. Samuel and Mary were lucky, as they had fifteen children, all of whom grew into adulthood, which was rare at the time. Nine of those children joined them in the family cemetery.

Regarding the myth of the "slave graves" on the outside of the cemetery, these graves were actually placed on the grounds before there was a gate leading into the cemetery. The gate was erected during the time of modern automobiles, and space was required for parking. Unfortunately, the graves of the Whitlatch family extended into what would become the parking area, and they were left outside of the gate. The earliest burial was that of an infant Whitlatch who passed away on April 28, 1891, followed by fifteen-year-old William Whitlatch the following month on May 30. Both of these children belonged to Peter B. and Catherine Elizabeth Sommerville Whitlatch, who are also buried on the grounds. Clearly, this is a family plot and not a location where hangings or slave burials took place. Visitors to the cemetery might also note that there are several sunken spots, likely the location of graves that no longer have stones. Venturing to the back of the site, near the tree row, one will find a group of small, illegible tombstones, many of which have an American flag placed in the ground beside them. These memorials belong to the many soldiers who are buried in Bridgewater Cemetery, many of them likely dating to the Civil War.

The long history and remote location of Bridgewater Cemetery has made it a favorite stop for teenagers and ghost hunters alike. There have been reports of cult activity in the cemetery, with visitors encountering strange individuals and, in some instances, discovering the charred remains of dissected animals on the grounds. The site has long been reported by locals to be haunted, with many people claiming that it could be one of the most haunted locations in the state. EVPs have been recorded on numerous occasions on the grounds, with investigators claiming to have made contact with several different spirits, including those of a woman and

Right: Entrance to Bridgewater Cemetery.

Below: Tombstone of Samuel and Mary Ann Bridgewater at Bridgewater Cemetery.

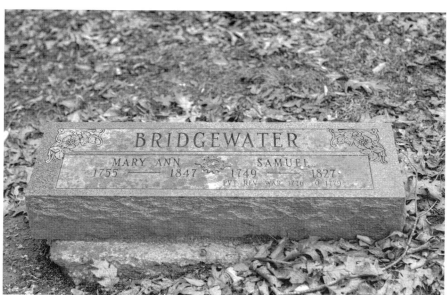

Above: Whitlatch graves at Bridgewater Cemetery.

Left: Child's grave at Bridgewater Cemetery.

various children. Orbs and ectoplasmic activity have been photographed on numerous occasions when no activity was visible to the naked eye. Some visitors have felt as though they were touched or felt a warm breath on the back of their neck. Visitors have also experienced sounds in the cemetery that they cannot explain. Strange whistling has been heard, along with yelling and screaming, the sound of laughter and even the galloping of horses. Visitors have also reported seeing a man on horseback, though he never interacts with those in the cemetery. Sometimes it appears that he is missing his head. A riderless white horse has been seen on the grounds. When approached, it will either disappear or run at full speed toward those who have witnessed it. The apparition of a night watchman, as well as that of a gentleman in a white hat, have been reported in the area.

Perhaps the most active location seems to be the tree row near the Civil War–era graves. This is where an entity known as "Red Eyes" has been encountered. Reports state that as you venture to the back of the cemetery, the temperature will drop quickly, and the tombstones nearby seem to glow. That is when you can expect to encounter Red Eyes. You will suddenly feel as though you are being watched, and then you will see them, a pair of beady red eyes, sometimes peering from behind a tombstone and other times watching from just inside the tree row. A black figure, almost mist-like, has also been seen moving about in this area. Even when attempting to leave the cemetery, visitors have experienced things that they cannot explain. Upon returning to their vehicles, people have seen handprints on the windows of their cars. Vehicles that seemed to be functioning properly before people entered the cemetery seemed to stall and not start. Small black objects have also been seen bouncing around vehicles as visitors attempt to exit the grounds. One thing is certain: when visiting Bridgewater Cemetery, never go alone and always be prepared for an encounter with one of the many supernatural beings believed to inhabit this spooky location.

14

BLACKFOOT CEMETERY

300 East County Road 900 South, Oakland City, IN 47660
Gibson County
Hours: Dawn until dusk

Blackfoot Cemetery is in a rather isolated location, peacefully tucked away on a lonely country road. The cemetery has been in use since the 1800s, with many of the burials belonging to the first settlers of Gibson and Pike Counties. However, it is believed that some of the residents were placed there before the site became a proper burial ground; the location of their burials is therefore unknown. It is reported that the first unmarked grave in the cemetery is that of a woman. She belonged to a caravan of settlers passing through the area on its way to Illinois. Fortunately, the group came into contact with a tribe of Native Americans, said to be Blackfoot, and they helped the caravan find a suitable location to bury the woman. They chose a quiet spot at the top of a hill, not far from a small log church. It is likely that this story would have occurred prior to 1800. At that time, there is no record of any Blackfoot villages in Indiana. However, there were other groups in the area that could have offered support to the mourning settlers. The most probable seems to be the Delaware Indians, as they had two settlements in proximity to the current location of Blackfoot Cemetery and were known to frequent the area. These settlements also included many members of the Nanticoke tribe, which had migrated westward with the Delaware Indians. Some of these Nanticoke could have been from an area known as "Blackfoot

Town" in present-day Dagsboro, Delaware, hence the Blackfoot connection to the cemetery.

In the years following the first burial, parishioners continued to gather at the site of the small church, now called Blackfoot Church, but is wasn't until John Almon began homesteading the land that a proper cemetery was placed on the grounds. According to a memorial marker at the site, the first burial in the cemetery was that of Mrs. John Almon. However, it seems unlikely that John's wife, Hollan, is the first recorded burial in Blackfoot Cemetery, as she passed away on July 23, 1874, many years after the cemetery was established. John's mother, Mary Sansum Almon, who died on September 11, 1844, is also buried in the cemetery and, according to records, is the first resident of Blackfoot Cemetery. Even more interesting is that John himself passed away on December 27, 1856, nearly twenty years before the death of his wife. It is possible that both John and his mother could have been buried elsewhere and were later moved to their current resting places. It seems more likely that early historical records confused the two Mrs. Almons, attributing the earlier burial to Hollan, when in fact it was Mary.

A new church was built on the site in 1860 to accommodate the growing congregation and the many new burials coming into the cemetery. That church stood for thirty-six years until it was destroyed by a storm, paving the way for the third and final Blackfoot church constructed on the grounds. That church was finished in 1897 and remained on the property for nearly one hundred years. Sadly, as is often the case with old burial grounds and abandoned buildings, vandals took their toll on the site, damaging the Blackfoot church beyond repair. In 1991, a meeting was held to discuss the building's future. In the end, the old church was demolished in the winter of 1991 and had been fully removed from the cemetery by February 1992.

In the years that the church stood empty, strange rumors began to circulate about the once serene location. Teenagers and adults alike told tales of satanists using the area for vile and wicked rituals. Later, it was claimed

Illegible grave at Blackfoot Cemetery.

that the church had actually burned, leaving nothing but ash behind. There are also stories of a "Witch's Grave," though no exact location is given. It is said to stand alone, far from any other residents. However, when wandering through the cemetery, it is quite difficult to single out one grave that appears to stand alone. It is possible that the grave itself is no longer there or that this is a myth that has circulated throughout the years.

Visitors to the cemetery have also reported ghostly activity throughout the grounds, including the sensation of being watched and ghost lights that seem to appear regularly, often with no cars present on the road. Full-body apparitions have been witnessed, and many people claim to have photographed orbs and other anomalies. One of the more chilling accounts is that of disembodied voices and unidentifiable sounds that can be heard throughout the cemetery and in the woods nearby. But, upon further investigation, the source cannot be identified. The reported activity seems to suggest that some of what is being experienced is residual energy remaining from the more than two hundred years of human interaction at the site. One can't help but envision the spirits of the Delaware Indians, mingling with the early parishioners of the Blackfoot church, still behaving as they did in life.

15

Springdale Cemetery

600 West Fifth Street, Madison, IN 47250
Jefferson County
Hours: Daily, 8:00 a.m. to 4:00 p.m.
Website: https://www.nps.gov/nr/travel/madison/Springdale_
Cemetery.html

Springdale Cemetery is the oldest active burial ground in Madison. Before it, many of Madison's residents were buried on the south side of Crooked Creek in what was referred to as the Third Street Cemetery, or Old City Cemetery. However, as one can imagine, with the cemetery being near the creek, it was subject to flooding, and often, the bodies of those buried there would rise from their graves, causing concern among the living. It was soon decided that a second cemetery was needed. A location was selected on the northwest side of Crooked Creek, where Fifth Street ends, far enough from the creek to alleviate any concerns of flooding. Springdale Cemetery opened its gates in 1839. Springdale is a European-inspired rural cemetery with stone-lined drainage ditches, likely a precautionary measure considering the previous issues with flooding. There is also a beautiful Gothic Revival chapel, complete with stained-glass windows. It was added to the grounds in 1916 by architect Frederick Wallick.

The first recorded burial was that of Frances "Fanny" Sullivan, who died at the age of fifteen on October 7, 1839. She was the daughter of well-known Madison judge Jeremiah Sullivan, who once sat on the Indiana

Above: Original entrance to Springdale Cemetery.

Left: Chapel at Springdale Cemetery.

Grave of Fannie Sullivan. Hers was the first burial at Springdale Cemetery.

Supreme Court and is thought to have coined the name *Indianapolis* for the state capital. Judge Sullivan and his wife, Charlotte, had thirteen children, eight of them growing into adulthood. Three of Fanny's siblings passed while still infants, and her younger sister Julia was only six at the time of her death. Fanny's grave can be found in section one, lot fourteen. She is buried with both of her parents and eight of her siblings. The Sullivan family home still stands on Second Street in Madison, along with many of the city's early nineteenth-century homes. The residence is reported to have its fair share of ghostly activity, and visitors to the city can take guided tours of the Sullivan home from April to October.

Springdale Cemetery received an influx of new residents in 1859 and again in 1904, when bodies and tombstones were moved from the Third Street Cemetery. In 1859, the first move brought many of the residents from the old cemetery across Crooked Creek to their new home at Springdale Cemetery. However, there was concern that perhaps not everyone had been relocated. Many bodies had washed away in earlier floods, and some paupers' graves had never had monuments to begin with. There was also talk of a vault where the bodies of infants and those who had escaped their flooded graves were laid to rest. In 1904, the Daughters of the American Revolution renovated the old burial ground into the John Paul Park. Remaining stones were taken to Springdale Cemetery to join those that had been moved years earlier. The former residents of the Third Street Cemetery can now be found grouped together in an area known as the Old Public Grounds section. The area south of Crooked Creek still serves as the home of John Paul Park, with many visitors reporting strange activity on the grounds, including orbs and cold spots. One can't help but wonder if these are the souls of those left behind so many years ago.

Springdale Cemetery is also home to many notable burials and monuments. Several Civil War veterans are buried there, including Alois O. Bachman Jr., who served as a Union army officer and lieutenant colonel of the Nineteenth Indiana Volunteer Infantry and the Iron Brigade, an infantry unit that fought in the eastern theater during the war. He was killed on September 17, 1862, during the Battle of Antietam in Maryland. He is buried in section 1, lot 130. Rear Admiral Napoleon Collins is another notable military serviceman buried on the grounds. He was a veteran of both the Mexican-American War and the Civil War, having served with the Union. He continued to serve until his death on August 9, 1875, in Callao, Peru. He had been in command of a South Pacific squadron at the time. He is buried beneath a tall monument adorned with an anchor in lot 430, plat 5. Fans of the St. Louis Cardinals may also recognize the tombstone of Tommy Thevenow, a shortstop and leading hitter who helped the Cardinals win the 1926 World Series. He played with several other teams, including the Philadelphia Phillies and the Cincinnati Reds, out-hitting fellow big-name players such as Babe Ruth, Lou Gehrig and Tony Lazzeri. Following his retirement from baseball, Thevenow moved home to Madison and opened a grocery store. He died of a cerebral hemorrhage on July 29, 1957, and was buried in lot 422, not far from the cemetery's chapel.

The most famous monument in Springdale Cemetery is near an area at the back of the cemetery known as Hanging Rock Hill. It is a large, Italian marble sculpture of a woman, her arms outstretched toward the sky. The monument was created by George Gray Barnard in 1922 for his family's plot. He titled the statue *Let There Be Light* and placed it overlooking the graves of his parents, Dr. Joseph and Martha Barnard. The family originally lived in Kankakee, Illinois, but moved to Madison when Joseph was offered the position of minister at the Madison Second Presbyterian Church. By the time the family moved to Indiana, George was twenty years old and attending the École nationale supérieure des Beaux-Arts in Paris, France. He would go on to showcase his sculptures throughout the United States and the world. He had three siblings, only one of whom was born in Madison, a sister named Martha, in honor of their mother. None of the children is buried in the family plot; George's final resting place is the Harrisburg Cemetery in Harrisburg, Pennsylvania. In the years since George added the statue to the site, it has become known not just for its beauty but also for the ghostly activity associated with it. It has long been reported that if one visits the cemetery on Easter morning, they will most certainly witness tears of blood falling from the woman's eyes. For those who have disobeyed the posted visiting hours and entered the cemetery at night, the stories take a much darker turn. It is said that if one kisses the feet of the statue, it will enrage the spirit within, causing the statue to come to life and leap from its pedestal, chasing the poor soul that dare sully its feet with their lips.

Balls of light have also been reported to bounce about in the cemetery, with many people stating that headlights could not be the cause, as Fifth Street dead-ends at the cemetery. Others state that these balls of light move far too quickly to be caused by artificial light. Cold spots are another common occurrence, felt on even the warmest of evenings. Visitors have also reported hearing a variety of strange sounds while in the cemetery at night. However, it is important to note that many animals also frequent the area and could account for odd sounds in the cemetery.

Above: Thomas Thevenow grave at Springdale Cemetery.

Right: *Let There Be Light* sculpture at Springdale Cemetery.

Perhaps some of the supernatural activity in the cemetery can be attributed to a flood that occurred in 1978. Despite the location of Springdale Cemetery, it was not immune to the rising waters of Crooked Creek. During the 1978 flood, several residents of the cemetery rose from their long sleep, still encased in their coffins. Many floated into the creek, with volunteers scurrying to retrieve as many of Springdale's inhabitants as possible. However, upon returning to the cemetery, the volunteers found it nearly impossible to return the coffins to their original graves, as there was obviously no identifying information available. Instead, they began placing coffins in the open graves until all of them had been reburied. Because of this, it is likely that some of the tombstones do not match the identity of the person buried beneath them. Visitors to the cemetery often report seeing what appears to be a person walking among the rows of tombstones, swinging a lantern. The torso and legs of the individual are always visible, but the arms and face are bathed in blackness. Could this be the spirit of one of the volunteers, possibly attempting to find displaced souls? Or is it one of many unsettled spirits forced to eternally wander the cemetery in search of its original grave site?

16

BONDS CHAPEL CEMETERY

8070 COUNTY ROAD 810 NORTH, WEST BADEN SPRINGS, IN 47469
ORANGE COUNTY
HOURS: DAWN UNTIL DUSK
HTTPS://WWW.FACEBOOK.COM/PG/BONDSCHAPELUMC/ABOUT/?REF=PAGE_
INTERNAL

Bonds Chapel is a small cemetery tucked away in the Hoosier National Forest. It is accompanied by a rural Methodist church that welcomes congregants to this day. It is believed that the land was once known as the Old Webb Place and contained the first log church to be built on the grounds. The land later belonged to a Reverend John W. Bond, a Methodist preacher and likely one of the earliest men of God to give a sermon on the grounds. The Bonds Chapel Cemetery was in use during the time that Reverend Bond owned the land, with the first burial being of a man named Duncan Dickey, who passed away in 1849. In the years since his death, a new tombstone has been erected to include not only Duncan but also his wife, Almeda, and their son Duncan C. Dickey and his wife, Florence. Reverend Bond is also buried on the grounds, having passed away on February 28, 1857, at the age of eighty-one. He was preceded in death by his wife, Alles, who is buried next to him. Following his death, his son John N. Bond donated the land for continued use as a church and cemetery. The land continues to function in that capacity to this day. In the years since the reverend's passing, this otherwise serene cemetery has become a favorite site for those interested in legends and the supernatural.

Grave of Reverend John Bond at Bonds Chapel Cemetery.

Visitors to the cemetery often tell of experiencing strange activity while on the grounds. Some visitors have reported that the tombstones seem to change shape at night and that apparitions often appear among the stones before vanishing. Orbs have been photographed in the cemetery, and a strange light has been witnessed floating throughout the church when no congregants are in the building. Many people have reported seeing a woman dressed in black, both in the cemetery and standing across the street. Those who have witnessed this apparition claim that she has a link to a specific grave located on the grounds.

Upon entering the cemetery, one may not initially notice the grave of Floyd E. Pruett, but locals are well versed in the story of this strange tombstone. If one steps close to Floyd's grave, they will surely notice what appears to be the indentations from a chain on the left side of the stone. Many people claim that the links continue to grow with each passing year. But what could cause such a strange phenomenon? There are many stories to account for the existence of the chain indentations on Floyd's grave, but could any of them be true? One of the earliest stories claims that Floyd was a slave and was beaten to death with a chain, but that doesn't seem to add up, as Floyd passed away in 1920 and his grave clearly states that he served in the military. Another frequently circulated story posits that Floyd was called to service during World War I, leaving behind a heartbroken girlfriend. Floyd was killed in battle, and his body was returned to Indiana for the funeral. During his burial, his girlfriend wept as she stood across the road from the cemetery. It is said that the woman in black is Floyd's long-lost love still mourning his death and that the chain continues to grow to this day as a symbol of her love for him.

Perhaps the most well-known story of Floyd E. Pruett is that he was a logger in Orleans, Indiana. He was happily married to his wife, Sara, before being called to serve in World War I. Upon returning from Europe in 1918, Floyd was reportedly a changed man. He had long belonged to the Protestant faith, while Sara was a practicing Catholic, and once he returned home, Sara's religious beliefs became an item of contention for the couple. It is also said that during Floyd's time away, Sara had befriended a local gentleman who also belonged to the Catholic Church and that this could have caused some jealousy on Floyd's behalf. Whatever the cause of their issues, Sara was soon found dead in a remote wooded area not far from Orleans. A chain was tightly pulled around her neck, and the cause of death was deemed to be strangulation. Locals immediately rallied around Floyd, assuming that he could never be guilty of such a heinous crime. Sara's family was convinced

Grave of Floyd Pruett at Bonds Chapel Cemetery. Note the indentation of a chain on the side of the tombstone.

otherwise, claiming that Floyd had changed dramatically since returning from the war. Eventually, it became obvious to Sara's family that with so much support in the community, Floyd would never be arrested or punished for the crime. The family then relied on their Catholic faith and prayed heavily that Floyd would one day do the penance that he deserved. Two years to the day after Sara's murder, Floyd was working as a logger once again, but on this day, he finally received the punishment that Sara's family had prayed for when a tree that he was cutting fell the wrong way, landing directly on Floyd and killing him instantly. Floyd was buried in Bonds Chapel Cemetery. No one reported anything strange about his tombstone at the time. However, one year later, on what was also the third anniversary of Sara's death, visitors to Floyd's grave stated that something about the tombstone was different; there was now the indentation of a chain, perhaps the very one that Floyd had used to kill Sara. In an alternate version of the story, it is said that while being strangled with a chain, Sara used her last dying breath to put a curse on Floyd, ensuring that he, too, would suffer for her murder. It was only a few days following the discovery of Sara's body that Floyd lost his life in a freak accident. He was working near a timber wagon when one of the chains broke loose. It whipped violently through the air, finding Floyd and snapping his neck.

In the years since, visitors to Bonds Chapel Cemetery claim that the chain markings on Floyd's stone seem to grow longer with each passing anniversary of Sara's murder and that the tombstone itself is cursed, with anyone who touches the chain dying not long after. Some have even reported that an eerie glow seems to emit from the chain at night. Others believe that the lady in black of Bonds Chapel Cemetery is none other than Sara Pruett and that she remains there to ensure that Floyd never rests peacefully and that he will be eternally punished for her murder. The apparition of a man has also been spotted on the grounds on a few occasions, leading some to believe that it is Floyd, still cursed for Sara's murder.

In truth, there is likely a very simple explanation for how the chain indentations came to be on Floyd's grave. Some believe that while the stone used for his monument was still in the quarry, it may have come in contact with a rusty chain that left its mark on the tombstone. Others believe that a chain was once draped over the monument and that, after the metal oxidized, it left a permanent stain on the tombstone. Floyd was married and he was a military veteran. However, his wife's name was not Sara, but Edna Wolter Pruett. They lived in Ohio for a time and, by all accounts, remained happily married until his death. Floyd was also not employed as a logger. Rather, he worked in the limestone quarries of southern Indiana. It is said that Floyd contracted tuberculosis and passed away not long after being diagnosed with the disease. Edna then left Orange County to return to Hamilton, Ohio, where she married a man named Edward Galt. Following Edward's death, Edna moved to Georgia and is buried in Floral Hills Memory Garden in Tucker, Georgia, along with her sister Alma. As for the apparitions encountered on the grounds, perhaps these are some of the early parishioners of the small country church, still attending services to this day.

Interestingly, there is a very similar story to Floyd's that takes place in nearby Pulaski County, Kentucky. Even stranger is the name of the man: Carl Pruitt. Though they are not believed to be related, Carl's stone is said to be emblazoned with the mark of a chain, and locals state that it continues to grow every year. It is also said that Carl used a chain to murder his wife. Then, after realizing the gravity of the act, he turned a gun on himself. However, there seems to be no record of Carl Pruitt or his grave site beyond the story circulated online. It seems likely that the story of Floyd Pruett made its way farther south and somehow morphed into the story of Carl Pruitt, as has happened with many urban legends. That being said, one can only judge the story of Floyd Pruett and the ghostly activity at Bonds Chapel Cemetery by visiting for one's self.

17

STEPP CEMETERY

5006 EAST MAIN FOREST ROAD, BENTON TOWNSHIP, IN 46151
MONROE COUNTY
HOURS: DAILY 8:00 A.M. TO 10:00 P.M.

Stepp Cemetery in the Morgan-Monroe State Forest near Bloomington, Indiana, is a hauntingly beautiful location tucked away in a small, almost circular clearing, accessible only by a small dirt walking path. The cemetery is considered a rural farm cemetery, as many of its inhabitants were involved with early agriculture in the area. The land was originally owned by the cemetery's namesake, Reuben Stepp, who purchased the land, including the established cemetery, in 1856. Stepp owned the land for twenty-eight years before selling it to Will Peterson in 1884, who sold the land to the State of Indiana in 1929. There are roughly fifty tombstones remaining in the cemetery, with the earliest monuments dating to 1851. The first burial is that of Private Isaac Hartsock, a veteran of the War of 1812. Years of disrepair and vandalism have taken their toll on many of the tombstones, so it is quite likely that additional burials are hidden in the cemetery.

Stepp Cemetery is considered by many to be one of the most haunted cemeteries in Indiana, with paranormal activity reportedly occurring at the site since the 1800s. One of the earliest ghostly tales involves one of Reuben Stepp's children. Apparently, there was a property disagreement within the family that led to the death of Reuben's son. Not being able to rest, his spirit is reported to angrily roam the cemetery, confronting anyone who dares

Above: Stepp Cemetery sign.

Left: Grave of Isaac Hartsock at Stepp Cemetery.

Grave of Reuben Stepp at Stepp Cemetery.

trespass on the property that he coveted in life. In truth, Reuben Stepp had seventeen children with his wife, Sabra, but none of those children appears to be buried in Stepp Cemetery. However, Reuben is buried there, along with his infant grandson, Thomas Stepp, who died in 1869 at one year and twenty-seven days old.

A similar version of this story states that the land was originally owned by a family, presumably in the years prior to Reuben Stepp's ownership of the land. When the patriarch of the family passed, he did not specify which of his two sons would receive the land at his death, which sowed discord between the brothers. The confrontation came to a fatal conclusion on the ground that is now Stepp Cemetery, with the brothers deciding to face off in a duel. The winner would receive their father's land. Unfortunately, both brothers were reportedly losers that day, as the two bullets that were fired fatally struck their intended targets, killing both brothers. Currently, there are no graves in the cemetery that correspond to two brothers having been buried there in the same year. Assuming they would have likely been the first interments at Stepp Cemetery, perhaps their markers have been lost to time.

Over the years, many stories have circulated regarding a strange religious cult, referred to as the "Crabbites." They were inspired by the Book of Revelation and believed that Earth was square. Some legends state that members of the group, who were also believed to participate in snake-handling and free love, are buried in the cemetery. Religious groups such as these have been found in areas of rural Appalachia and are often somewhat secretive and isolated. The terrain of the Morgan-Monroe State Forest is very similar to that of Appalachia, so it is possible that this is what attracted the Crabbites to the area. The cult was supposedly located near Stepp Cemetery, and its members often used the grounds to carry out bizarre rituals. It is said that the group was led by a single leader and that the members spoke in tongues, handled snakes and danced naked among the tombstones. These rituals often included the rather gruesome addition of sacrificing small animals, after which the members imbibed in various intoxicating beverages and participated in gratuitous orgies before disappearing into the night. This behavior likely left its mark on the hallowed grounds of Stepp Cemetery, possibly contributing to the existence of dark entities and the many reports of paranormal activity in this otherwise peaceful location. Some visitors to the cemetery have reported seeing a woman in a long white dress, likely similar to one that may have been worn by followers of the Crabbites. She is often seen walking slowly through the trees surrounding the cemetery, but once she is bathed in light, her form changes to that of something dark and ominous before disappearing from sight.

The most commonly reported spirit at Stepp Cemetery is that of the woman in black. There are many different stories surrounding this apparition, but they all have one thing in common: the loss of a child. She is often seen sitting, shrouded in black, on a tree stump near the back of the cemetery grounds. When approached, she will either disappear or dash into the woods. Her spirit has also been seen walking slowly among the trees before vanishing. Other witnesses report seeing the lady in black bent over, almost as if she is digging for something in the cemetery. Many visitors have reported that the spirit can sometimes be seen crying as she sits on the stump, while others have heard her mournful cries, myself included. On an evening visit to the cemetery, we were greeted by teenagers using a Ouija board. It is an activity that I do not recommend. Following their departure, we continued to walk around the cemetery near the path leading to our car when we began to hear a sound near the back of the cemetery that I can only describe as that of a woman weeping. We followed the sound past the stump and into the woods but heard it just once more. I can tell you that the sadness of that sound sent chills down my spine. Photos have also been taken of the woman in black, with the most famous clearly showing a somewhat transparent woman sitting on the stump. She is dressed in what appears to be dark clothing with a veil over her face. It is also said that if one sits on the stump during a full moon, they will be cursed to die in exactly one year.

The Crabbites are responsible for one of the many ghostly legends associated with the lady in black and the tree stump. It is said that one of the group's followers, a young mother named Anna, tragically lost her daughter in a hit-and-run accident on Indiana 37. Grief-stricken, she buried the child at Stepp Cemetery. But this is where the sad story takes a rather grisly turn. Anna returned the night after burying her child and carefully exhumed the body, cradling it in her arms before once again burying her daughter. She followed this same pattern night after night until, one evening, a tree near the grave was struck by lightning, leaving a large stump. This soon became a chair of sorts, where Anna, who was always dressed in black, could sit and rock her daughter before once again burying the child. Locals began referring to the stump as the "Warlock's Chair" and did so long after Anna had passed away. Some people claimed that the chair was cursed and that Anna's spirit remains in the cemetery to this day.

In another version of this story, Anna was a wife and mother. Her husband, Jacob, was killed in a quarry accident and buried in Stepp Cemetery. Anna reportedly turned all of her attention to their sixteen-year-old daughter, Emily, and became protective of the girl. When Emily was invited to a dance, Anna had her reservations but allowed her daughter to attend. The weather turned rainy that night. Returning home from the dance, the car with Emily and her date slid off the road, hitting a tree. Emily was killed instantly. Anna had her daughter buried in Stepp Cemetery next to Jacob. Anna visited Emily's grave every day and was often seen by locals, draped in black, sitting on the large stump and speaking to her daughter as if she were still alive. Much as with the previous tale, the sorrowful spirit of Anna is said to remain in the cemetery, mourning the loss of her daughter. There is potentially some truth to this tale, as there is a Jacob and Anna Adkins buried in Stepp Cemetery. The couple had eleven children, one of whom, Ida Mae, passed away at the age of seventeen. She was buried in Frye Cemetery, also known as Taylor or McGowan Cemetery, located on North Low Gap Road in the Morgan-Monroe State Forest, not far from Stepp Cemetery.

The final version of the tale of the woman in black seems to surround not only the tree stump but also a small, flat gravestone with yellow lettering emblazoned with the name "Baby Lester" and the year "1937." Baby Lester is buried near the Adkins family plot at the back of the cemetery, not far

Grave of Baby Lester at Stepp Cemetery.

from the tree stump. You cannot miss his stone, as it is often covered in gifts, including coins and toys, from visitors to his grave. It is said that, following the death of her days-old son, Baby Lester's mother began coming to the cemetery to mourn the loss of her child. She would often be seen dressed in black and sitting on the stump. Following her death, her spirit remained in the cemetery and has been seen there ever since. In truth, Baby Lester passed away after taking only a few breaths in 1937. His mother, Olethia Pryor Lester, and father, Harley Lester, eventually divorced. Olethia later married James Walls and moved to Indianapolis. It is unlikely that Olethia is the woman in black, as she lived to be eighty-five years old, passing away in 2007, long after the reports of the woman in black began. She is buried in Oaklawn Memorial Gardens in Fishers, Indiana.

Despite the fact that Baby Lester is likely not the infant associated with the woman in black, that does not entirely debunk the myth. Many of the burials in Stepp Cemetery, including those of Thomas Stepp and Baby Lester, are of infants and children. The Hacker family also has many members buried in the cemetery, including the children of Sir Malcom Dunbar Hacker and his wife, Annie, both of whom are buried there. They had eight children, including Estella, Isaac and Orestes, all of whom died before reaching the age of seven. The remaining five children in the family, some of whom lived only into their twenties, are also buried in Stepp Cemetery. One has to wonder if the stories of a mourning mother named Anna could actually refer to the ghost of Annie Hacker, who may have returned to the cemetery to mourn the loss of her three young children. There is also some debate as to whether the large tree stump currently in the cemetery is the one associated with the woman in black, or if that stump disintegrated long ago and returned to the earth, being replaced with a stump from another of the many felled trees in the cemetery.

There are reports of additional spirits known to wander Stepp Cemetery. The spirit of a teenage girl has been seen in the cemetery on numerous occasions. It is said that, sometime in the 1950s, she was murdered in the Morgan-Monroe State Forest and her body dumped near the cemetery. Some stories state that she had been decapitated. Her mother spent the remainder of her life trying to find the killer but failed. It is said that the ghost of the girl now wanders the cemetery, perhaps seeking the justice that escaped her mother or, possibly, searching for her own lost head. Though many reports state that the murder occurred in the 1950s, it is quite possible that this story began to circulate as a result of the high-profile murder of Indiana University student Ann Harmeier in 1977. Ann was reported missing after she did not arrive for class as expected. Her car was later found on Indiana 37, two miles from Martinsville. It had overheated due to a faulty thermostat. After an extensive search that lasted thirty-six days, Ann's body was found in a cornfield roughly seven miles northeast of Martinsville. She is buried in Milton Cemetery in Milton, Indiana. Her killer has not been brought to justice.

Stepp Cemetery is also home to an urban legend similar to the Hookman of Tillett Cemetery. In this case, it is a Hookwoman, who was once a grieving mother. As the story goes, the mother was driving with her son on Indiana 37 when they were in an accident. The young boy was killed instantly and later buried in Stepp Cemetery. His mother survived, but her hand had been severed during the accident, later being replaced with a hook. Her son had been afraid of the dark in life, so the mother ventured to the cemetery nightly to watch over her son's grave. It is said that, even in death, she returns to the cemetery to comfort her son and will reportedly chase off trespassers while waving her hook angrily at them.

Aside from the many specters believed to inhabit Stepp Cemetery, the location also has its fair share of other paranormal activity. Visitors report seeing dark shadows moving about, and they sometimes report being followed by these shadows. Footsteps and whispers have been heard throughout the cemetery when no one else is present. Orbs and ectoplasmic mist have been caught on camera on several occasions, as witnessed by the photographer and myself during our visit to the cemetery to conduct research for this book. Those who claim to be sensitive to the supernatural tend to feel a sense of melancholy when visiting. Reports of strange smells, including of flowery perfumes and of something rancid or mildewed, have been experienced throughout the cemetery. There have also been Sasquatch sightings in the Morgan-Monroe State Forest near a hiking trail that crosses the path leading to the cemetery. Reports indicate that the creature is eight feet tall with thick black fur, leading some to wonder if the foul smell reported in the cemetery could be linked to this beast.

Visitors to the cemetery have also encountered strange men wearing white cloaks in the woods around the cemetery. But by all accounts, these men are not ghosts. It is reported that they have also been seen carrying a strange book and have sometimes even told witnesses that they are attempting to conjure the devil. In other instances, they have quietly followed hikers on the trails near the cemetery, causing quite a bit of concern to those who have encountered them. Stories of these men continue to circulate, with the most recent report occurring in 2010. Could these men be a modern-day version of the Crabbites, or possibly devil worshippers drawn to the cemetery due to its dark history and ghostly lore? It is hard to tell, but one thing is certain: when visiting the cemetery, always be aware of your surroundings and never visit the cemetery after closing time, as you will be truly alone with the inhabitants of Stepp Cemetery, whomever they may be.

BIBLIOGRAPHY

America's Most Haunted. "Who Killed Pearl Bryan and Where Is Her Head?" Accessed September 2019. www.americas-most-haunted.com.

Angelfire. "Bridgewater Cemetery—Scottsburg, Indiana." Accessed August 2019. www.angelfire.com.

———. "Springdale Cemetery—Madison, Indiana." Accessed November 2019. http://www.angelfire.com.

———. "The Tell-Tale Tombstone." Accessed November 2019. http://www.angelfire.com.

Are You Terrified? "Mother of a Ghost Story: Stepp Cemetery." Accessed November 2019. http://areyouterrified.blogspot.com

Astonishing Legends. "Stepp Cemetery." Accessed November 2019. https://www.astonishinglegends.com.

Baker, Ronald L. *Hoosier Folk Legends.* Bloomington: Indiana University Press, 1982.

Bella Morte. "Crown Hill Cemetery." Accessed July 2019. https://www.bellamorte.net.

Biography. "Belle Gunness." Accessed October 2019. https://www.biography.com.

Bonds Chapel UMC. "About Page." Facebook. Accessed November 2019. https://www.facebook.com.

Bridgehunter. "Houck Covered Bridge, 14-67-11." Accessed September 2019. https://bridgehunter.com.

The Cemeteries of Miami County. "Tillett's Cemetery." Accessed August 2019. http://thecemeteriesofmiamicounty.blogspot.com.

Cemetery Stories. "The Murder of Pearl Bryan." Accessed September 2019. https://cemeterystories.wordpress.com.

Chicago Tribune. "A Century-Old Mystery: Did Serial Killer Fake Her Death?" February 12, 2008. https://www.chicagotribune.com.

———. "Hell's Belle." March 1, 1987. https://www.chicagotribune.com.

CNN. "Indiana Approves Plan to Exhume John Dillinger's Grave on New Year's Eve." Accessed November 2019. https://www.cnn.com.

Crown Hill Funeral Home and Cemetery. "Tours." Accessed July 2019. https://www.crownhill.org.

Crown Hill Heritage Foundation. "Lucy Ann Seaton." Accessed November 2019. https://crownhillhf.org.

The Cub. "Bridgewater Cemetery Beckons with the Thrill of Paranormal Activity." October 28, 2010. https://shscub.wordpress.com.

Cult Nation. "Anatomy of a Ghost Story: The Search for Carl Pruitt." Accessed November 2019. https://cultnation.com.

The DePauw. "Beer, Liquor and Spirits: DePauw's Ghostly Stories." October 24, 2017. https://thedepauw.com.

———. "Greencastle Ghost Stories." October 30, 2012. https://thedepauw.com.

The Enquirer. "120-Year-Old Beheading Still Fascinates." February 8, 2016. https://www.cincinnati.com.

Enterprise. "Haunted Indiana." Accessed August 2019. https://www.enterprise.com.

Exemplore. "The Most Haunted Places in Indiana." Accessed November 2019. https://exemplore.com.

Family Search. "George Carpenter." Accessed August 2019. https://www.familysearch.org.

———. "Horace J. Crismond." Accessed September 2019. https://www.familysearch.org.

———. "Jacob Ewald." Accessed September 2019. https://www.familysearch.org.

———. "Moses Boone." Accessed September 2019. https://www.familysearch.org.

———. "Peter B. Whitlatch." Accessed August 2019. https://www.familysearch.org.

———. "Phebe Rissler." Accessed September 2019. https://www.familysearch.org.

———. "Samuel Bridgewater." Accessed August 2019. https://www.familysearch.org.

———. "Squire Boone." Accessed September 2019. https://www.familysearch.org.

———. "Squire Boone, Jr." Accessed September 2019. https://www.familysearch.org.

———. "Susannah Boone." Accessed September 2019. https://www.familysearch.org.

———. "William O. Murdock." Accessed September 2019. https://www.familysearch.org.

Foulkes, Arthur. "Legend, Mystery, Folklore Part of Ghost Walk at ISU." *Tribune Star*, May 2, 2011. https://www.tribstar.com.

Fox News. "100-Year Mystery: Did 'Lady Bluebeard' Get Away with Murder?" April 27, 2008. https://www.foxnews.com.

Fun City Finder—Indianapolis, Indiana. "Justus Cemetery." Accessed October 2019. http://indianapolis-indiana.funcityfinder.com.

Geneaology.com. "Blackfoot Tribe in Kentucky." Accessed October 2019. https://www.genealogy.com.

Geocaching. "Boone's Place." Accessed September 2019. https://www.geocaching.com.

———. "Ewald Cemetery." Accessed September 2019. https://www.geocaching.com.

———. "Indiana Spirit Quest #399: Posey Chapel Cemetery." Accessed October 2019. https://www.geocaching.com.

The Ghost in My Machine. "Encyclopedia of the Impossible: 100 Steps Cemetery." Accessed August 2019. https://theghostinmymachine.com.

———. "Haunted Road Trip: The Morgan-Monroe State Forest, Stepp Cemetery, and the Lady in Black of Bloomington, Indiana." https://theghostinmymachine.com.

Ghost Research Society. "Posey Chapel and Cemetery Investigation." Accessed October 2019. https://ghostresearch.org.

Ghosts of America. "LaPorte, Indiana Ghost Pictures." Accessed October 2019. http://www.ghostsofamerica.com.

———. "Madison, Indiana Ghost Sightings." Accessed November 2019. www.ghostsofamerica.com.

———. "Oakland City, Indiana Ghost Pictures." Accessed October 2019. http://www.ghostsofamerica.com.

Ghost Study. "Pine Lake Cemetery and Its Ghosts." Accessed October 2019. http://www.ghoststudy.com.

A Grave Interest. "Haunted Blackfoot Cemetery." Accessed October 2019. agraveinterest.blogspot.com.

Gravely Speaking. "The Hoosier Poet." Accessed July 2019. https://gravelyspeaking.com.

Greencastle Banner Graphic. "Mail for Hamrick Station Bound for Dead Letter File." May 15, 1974. Vigo County Public Library. https://access.vigo.lib.in.us.

Greensburg Daily News. "History of the Pigeon Roost Massacre." June 22, 2016. https://www.greensburgdailynews.com.

Hamilton East Public Library. "Grave Robbing in Fishers—Part 3." Accessed September 2019. https://www.hepl.lib.in.us.

Haunted Places. "Blackfoot Cemetery." Accessed October 2019. https://www.hauntedplaces.org.

———. "Bonds Chapel Cemetery." Accessed November 2019. https://www.hauntedplaces.org.

———. "Boone-Hutcheson Cemetery." Accessed September 2019. https://www.hauntedplaces.org.

———. "Mount Hope Cemetery." Accessed September 2019. https://www.hauntedplaces.org.

———. "Posey Chapel." Accessed October 2019. https://www.hauntedplaces.org.

———. "Tillett Cemetery—Hookman's Cemetery." Accessed August 2019. https://www.hauntedplaces.org.

Haunted Places of Indiana. "Mount Hope Cemetery." Accessed September 2019. https://hauntedplacesofindiana.weebly.com.

Hawkins, Vance. "What Tribe Is the Eastern Blackfoot?" Vance Hawkins (blog), May 11, 2014. http://vancehawkins.blogspot.com.

Herald-Democrat. "Cemetery Board Is Appointed." September 10, 1915. https://newspapers.library.in.gov.

Herald Times. "Who Killed Ann Harmeier? Social Media Campaign Seeks to Solve a Murder 42 Years Later." September 22, 2019. https://www.hoosiertimes.com.

Historic Indianapolis. "The House of Blue Lights." Accessed February 2020. https://historicindianapolis.com.

———. "In the Park: Skiles Test Nature Park." Accessed February 2020. https://historicindianapolis.com.

Hoosier Happenings. "The Legend of Little Egypt." Accessed September 2019. hoosierhappenings.blogspot.com.

———. "Mt. Hope, Part 2." Accessed September 2019. hoosierhappenings.blogspot.com.

Hopkins, Marjorie. "Legends of the Valley." *Terre Haute Tribune Star*, October 13, 2013. https://www.tribstar.com.

House of Blue Lights. "Garry's Story." Accessed February 2020. houseofbluelights.com.

Hubpages. "Haunted Cemeteries in Indiana: Part One." Lori Gross (blog), October 19, 2016. https://hubpages.com.

Hunter, Al. "Gypsy Ghosts in Terry Hot." *Weekly View*, May 15, 2014. http://weeklyview.net.

Indiana Genealogy Trails. "Miami County Indiana—Charities and Cemeteries." Accessed August 2019. genealogytrails.com.

Indiana Ghost Detectives. "Hookmans Cemetery." Accessed August 2019. http://indianaghostdetectives.blogspot.com.

———. "Little Egypt." Accessed September 2019. http://indianaghostdetectives.blogspot.com.

———. "Mount Hope Cemetery." Accessed September 2019. http://indianaghostdetectives.blogspot.com.

———. "Patten Cemetery." Accessed October 2019. http://indianaghostdetectives.blogspot.com.

———. "Posey Chapel Cemetery." Accessed October 2019. http://indianaghostdetectives.blogspot.com.

———. "Scott County—Bridgewater Cemetery." Accessed August 2019. hoosierghost.proboards.com.

Indiana Haunted Houses. "Blackfoot Cemetery—Oakland City, IN." Accessed October 2019. https://www.indianahauntedhouses.com.

———. "Bridgewater Cemetery." Accessed August 2019. https://www.indianahauntedhouses.com.

Indiana Inside Blog. "Have a Hair-Raising Experience at the Most Haunted Cemetery in Indiana." Accessed August 2019. https://visitindiana.com.

Indianapolis Public Library. "Author Spotlight: James Whitcomb Riley." Accessed July 2019. https://www.indypl.org.

Indy Ghost Hunters. "Crown Hill Cemetery Indianapolis." Accessed July 2019. https://www.indyghosthunters.com.

INGenWebProject. "Beheaded by a Train—Friday December 3, 1880." Accessed August 2019. http://incass-inmiami.org.

———. "Blackfoot Cemetery." Accessed October 2019. ingenweb.org.

———. "Bonds Chapel Cemetery." Accessed November 2019. ingenweb.org.

———. "Cass County Cemetery History." Accessed September 2019. http://incass-inmiami.org.

———. "Patton Cemetery." Accessed October 2019. http://ingenweb.org.

———. "Pine Lake Cemetery." Accessed October 2019. ingenweb.org.

———. "Posey Chapel Cemetery Burials." Accessed October 2019. http://ingenweb.org.

———. "Scott County, Indiana Genealogy and History." Accessed August 2019. http://sites.rootsweb.com.

———. "Stepp Cemetery Benton Township—Section 9N." Accessed November 2019. http://ingenweb.org.

———. "Tillet Cemetery." Accessed August 2019. http://incass-inmiami.org.

Internet Archive. "History of Cass County, Indiana." Accessed September 2019. https://archive.org.

Jiffy Lube of Indiana. "5 Indiana Haunted Road Trips." Accessed August 2019. http://jiffylubeindiana.com.

Jorgensen, Virginia Dyer. *Ghosts of Madison, Indiana.* Charleston, SC: The History Press, 2012.

Kokomo Tribune. "Blasts from the Past." May 1, 2015. https://www.kokomotribune.com.

———. "The Scariest Things in the Woods Might Surprise You." July 27, 2018. https://www.kokomotribune.com.

LaPorte County Herald-Argus. "Discovering Pine Lake Cemetery." October 9, 2010. https://www.heraldargus.com.

———. "Patton Cemetery Can Be Spooky at 2 a.m." July 1, 2002. https://www.heraldargus.com.

LaPorte County Historical Society. "Belle Gunness." Accessed October 2019. https://laportecountyhistory.org.

Library of Congress. "About Peru Forester." Accessed August 2019. https://chroniclingamerica.loc.gov.

———. "About the Peru Gazette." Accessed August 2019. https://chroniclingamerica.loc.gov.

The Lost Chloe. "Madison, Indiana." Accessed November 2019. https://www.thelostchloe.com.

Malone, Dave. "Tales from the Campus Crypt." *State: The Magazine of Indiana State University*, October 1, 2014. http://statemagazine.com.

McCormick, Mike. "Anna M. Stewart Gains Notoriety for Her Communication with the Dead." *Terre Haute Tribune Star*, May 20, 2001.

———. *Terre Haute: Queen City of the Wabash.* Charleston, SC: Arcadia Publishing, 2005.

Mental Floss. "Six Seriously Spooky Cemetery Stories." Accessed November 2019. https://www.mentalfloss.com.

Michael C. Wells Photography. "Abandoned Bridgewater Cemetery." Accessed August 2019. www.michaelcwellsphotography.com.

Michigan City News-Dispatch. "LaPorte County's Top 10 Most Haunted." October 23, 2011. https://www.thenewsdispatch.com.

Mid-Western Ghosts and Hauntings. "The Headless Woman of Forest Hill Cemetery." Accessed September 2019. http://midwesternghostsandhauntings.blogspot.com.

Murderpedia. "Belle Sorenson Gunness." Accessed October 2019. https://murderpedia.org.

My Bloody Boneyards. "One Hundred Steps Cemetery." Accessed August 2019. https://vocal.media/horror/my-bloody-boneyards.

My Heritage. "Alois O. Bachman." Accessed October 2019. https://www.myheritage.com.

———. "Ann Hacker." Accessed November 2019. https://www.myheritage.com.

———. "Duncan Dickey." Accessed November 2019. https://www.myheritage.com.

———. "Edna A. Wolter Pruett Galt." Accessed November 2019. https://www.myheritage.com.

———. "Edward Galt." Accessed November 2019. https://www.myheritage.com.

———. "Floyd Elmer Pruett." Accessed November 2019. https://www.myheritage.com.

———. "Ida Mae Atkins." Accessed November 2019. https://www.myheritage.com.

———. "Jeremiah H. Sullivan." Accessed October 2019. https://www.myheritage.com.

———. "John Almon." Accessed October 2019. https://www.myheritage.com.

———. "John W. Bond." Accessed November 2019. https://www.myheritage.com.

———. "Malcolm Dunbar Hacker." Accessed November 2019. https://www.myheritage.com.

———. "Mary Samsun Almon." Accessed October 2019. https://www.myheritage.com.

———. "Reuben Stepp." Accessed November 2019. https://www.myheritage.com.

———. "Sabra Stepp." Accessed November 2019. https://www.myheritage.com.

————. "Thomas Stepp." Accessed November 2019. https://www.myheritage.com.

National Park Service. "John Paul Park." Accessed October 2019. https://www.nps.gov.

————. "Judge Jeremiah Sullivan House." Accessed October 2019. https://www.nps.gov.

————. "Springdale Cemetery." Accessed October 2019. https://www.nps.gov.

Nicklasch, Tanis. "Historical Treasure Santa Tried to Save Everyone in Horrific TH Fire in 1898." *Terre Haute Tribune Star*, December 16, 2018.

Notebook of Ghosts. "The Chain on the Tombstone." Accessed November 2019. https://notebookofghosts.com.

———— "Indiana Cemeteries Buswell and Justus." Accessed October 2019. https://notebookofghosts.com.

NUVO. "Grave Mistakes." June 28, 2006. https://www.nuvo.net.

————. "The Lesser-Known Residents of Crown Hill Cemetery." October 28, 2015. https://www.nuvo.net.

NWI Times. "Things that Go Bump in the Night." October 23, 2012. https://www.nwitimes.com.

The Odyssey Online. "11 Places to Visit Near Purdue University." Accessed September 2019. https://www.theodysseyonline.com.

Only in Your State. "The Story Behind This Haunted Cemetery in Indiana Is Truly Creepy." Accessed August 2019. https://www.onlyinyourstate.com.

Paranormal Realm. "100 Step Cemetery." Accessed August 2019. http://thephantomtribe.blogspot.com.

Pharos-Tribune. "Tracking Logansport's Lineage." Accessed September 2019. https://www.pharostribune.com.

Pocket Sights. "Springdale Cemetery—Madison's Treasures Tours." Accessed October 2019. https://pocketsights.com.

Pohlen, Jerome. *Oddball Indiana: A Guide to Some Really Strange Places.* Chicago: Chicago Review Press, 2002.

Putnam County Community Foundation. "Boone-Hutcheson Cemetery Endowment." Accessed September 2019. pcfoundation.org.

Reddit Indianapolis. "Local Ghost Stories?" Accessed July 2019. https://www.reddit.com.

Roadside Thoughts. "Peru, Indiana." Accessed August 2019. https://roadsidethoughts.com.

Rootsweb. "Cemeteries—German Township, Marshall County, Indiana—Ewald/Little Egypt." Accessed September 2019. http://sites.rootsweb.com.

———. "Patton Cemetery." Accessed October 2019. http://sites.rootsweb.com.

———. "Pine Lake Cemetery." Accessed October 2019. https://sites.rootsweb.com.

———. "Posey Chapel History." Accessed October 2019. https://sites.rootsweb.com.

Sally's Haunted Corridor. "Ghost Children—Forgotten Voices." Accessed July 2019. https://sites.google.com/site/hauntedcorridors.

Schlosser, S.E., and Paul G. Hoffman. *Spooky Indiana: Tales of Hauntings, Strange Happenings, and Other Local Lore.* Guilford, CT: Globe Pequot Press, 2012.

Southern Indiana Paranormal Investigations. "Bridgewater Cemetery." Accessed August 2019. http://southerninparanormal.blogspot.com.

Steemit. "The Legend of 100 Step Cemetery." Accessed August 2019. https://steemit.com.

Strange and Creepy. "Little Egypt Cemetery." Accessed September 2019. http://strangeandcreepy.com.

———. "100 Step Cemetery." Accessed August 2019. http://strangeandcreepy.com.

Terre Haute Saturday Spectator. "Death Notice of Martin Sheets." March 5, 1926.

———. "Tomb Telephones." April 3, 1926.

Terror Haute. "Martin Sheets." Accessed June 2019. http://www.terrorhaute.com.

This Is Indiana. "Justus Cemetery." Accessed October 2019. http://thisisindiana.angelfire.com.

TIPS. "Ewald Cemetery." Accessed September 2019. http://wearetips.exomagic.com.

Travel Channel. "Bobby Mackey's Haunted History." Accessed September 2019. https://www.travelchannel.com.

Tribune Star. "Final Resting Places: Where the Famous from Terre Haute Are Spending Eternity." October 31, 2010. https://www.tribstar.com.

———. "Valley Has Many Legends to Share." October 31, 2014. https://www.tribstar.com.

Unsolved Mysteries. "Bonds Chapel Cemetery—Indiana Ghosts." Accessed November 2019. unsolvedmysteries.com.

US Funks. "Bridgewater Family History." Accessed August 2019. https://www.usfunks.net.

Victorian Lives. "Logansport: A Historic Hoosier River Community." Accessed September 2019. http://victorianhousewives.blogspot.com.

Vigo County Historical Society. "Local Legends." Accessed June 2019. https://www.vchsmuseum.org.

Visit Indiana. "You Won't Believe the History Buried Beneath This Spot in Indy." Accessed July 2019. https://visitindiana.com.

Visit Indy. "James Whitcomb Riley Museum and Home." Accessed July 2019. https://www.visitindy.com.

Waymarking. "Justus Cemetery—Oxford, Indiana." Accessed October 2019. https://www.waymarking.com.

What's New LaPorte. "Final Resting Place? No So Much for Residents of LaPorte's Old City Cemetery." Accessed October 2019. https://whatsnewlaporte.com.

———. "Remains at LaPorte's Old City Cemetery Were Moved When Space Ran Out." Accessed October 2019. https://whatsnewlaporte.com.

Wikinut. "Paranormal Travels: Stepp Cemetery, Martinsville, Indiana." Accessed November 2019. https://guides.wikinut.com.

Willis, Wanda Lou Pohlen. *More Haunted Hoosier Trails: Folklore from Indiana's Spookiest Places*. Covington, KY: Clerisy Press, 2004.

Writers Café. "Southern Indiana Ghost Story." Accessed August 2019. https://www.writerscafe.org.

Find A Grave

Find A Grave. "Abinade Clarkson Patton, Memorial No. 76150416." https://www.findagrave.com/memorial/76150416/abinade-patton.

———. "Alfred Knobloch, Memorial No. 19589737." Accessed September 2019. https://www.findagrave.com/memorial/19589737/alfred-knobloch.

———. "Alma W. Hucke. Memorial No. 166990010." Accessed November 2019. https://www.findagrave.com/memorial/166990010/alma-hucke.

———. "Alois O. Bachman, Jr., Memorial No. 5900560." Accessed October 2019. https://www.findagrave.com/memorial/5900560/alois-o_-bachman.

———. "Andrew K. Helgelien, Memorial No. 26461302." Accessed October 2019. https://www.findagrave.com/memorial/26461302/andrew-k-helgelien.

———. "Annette C. Himmelberger Murdock, Memorial No 34819947." https://www.findagrave.com/memorial/34819947/annette-c-murdock.

———. "Annie E. Hacker, Memorial No. 9322356." Accessed November 2019. https://www.findagrave.com/memorial/9322356/annie-e_-hacker.

———. "Arthur Mack Grund, Memorial No. 34780626." Accessed September 2019. https://www.findagrave.com/memorial/34780626/arthur-mack-grund.

————. "Augustus Banks, Memorial No, 13608881." Accessed August 2019. https://www.findagrave.com/memorial/13608881/augustus-banks.

————. "Axel Sorenson, Memorial No. 93327993." Accessed October 2019. https://www.findagrave.com/memorial/93327993/axel-sorenson.

————. "Baby Lester, Memorial No. 17246514." Accessed November 2019. https://www.findagrave.com/memorial/17246514/baby-lester.

————. "Benjamin Harrison, Memorial No. 451." Accessed July 2019. https://www.findagrave.com/memorial/451/benjamin-harrison.

————. "Benjamin W. Peters, Memorial No. 34821581." Accessed September 2019. https://www.findagrave.com/memorial/34821581/benjamin-w-peters.

————. "Blackfoot Cemetery." Accessed October 2019. https://www.findagrave.com/cemetery/1979791/blackfoot-cemetery.

————. "Boone-Hutcheson Cemetery." Accessed September 2019. https://www.findagrave.com/cemetery/84393/boone-hutcheson-cemetery.

————. "Booth Tarkington, Memorial No. 1018." Accessed July 2019. https://www.findagrave.com/memorial/1018/booth-tarkington.

————. "Bridgewater Cemetery." Accessed August 2019. https://www.findagrave.com/cemetery/1467713/bridgewater-cemetery.

————. "Carol Albertson, Memorial No. 14182346." Accessed October 2019. https://www.findagrave.com/memorial/14182346/carol-albertson.

————. "Caroline Lavinia "Carrie" Scott Harrison, Memorial No. 3590." Accessed July 2019. https://www.findagrave.com/memorial/3590/caroline-lavinia-harrison.

————. "Caroline Sorenson, Memorial No. 93327921." Accessed October 2019. https://www.findagrave.com/memorial/93327921/caroline-sorenson.

————. "Carpenter's Cemetery." Accessed August 2019. https://www.findagrave.com/cemetery/2238877/carpenter-cemetery.

————. "Catherine Ewald, Memorial No. 19591664." Accessed September 2019. https://www.findagrave.com/memorial/19591664/catherine-ewald.

————. "Claude Herbert, Memorial No. 163586419." Accessed June 2019. https://www.findagrave.com/memorial/163586419/claude-herbert.

————. "Crown Hill Cemetery." Accessed July 2019. https://www.findagrave.com/cemetery/84781/crown-hill-cemetery.

————. "Daniel A. Boone, Memorial No. 11195251." Accessed September 2019. https://www.findagrave.com/memorial/11195251/daniel-a-boone.

————. "David Banks, Memorial No. 18575625." Accessed August 2019. https://www.findagrave.com/memorial/18575625/david-banks.

————. "Davidson Patton, Memorial No. 75804442." Accessed October 2019. https://www.findagrave.com/memorial/75804442/davidson-patton.

————. "Dr. Allen Pence, Memorial No. 28221717." Accessed September 2019. https://www.findagrave.com/memorial/28221717/allen-pence.

————. "Dr. John Ridpath, Memorial No. 13869035." Accessed September 2019. https://www.findagrave.com/memorial/13869035/john-clark-ridpath.

————. "Dr. John W. Crismond, Memorial No. 34644511." Accessed September 2019. https://www.findagrave.com/memorial/34644511/john-w-crismond.

————. "Dr. Joseph Hoke Barnard, Memorial No. 59311240." https://www.findagrave.com/memorial/59311240/joseph-hoke-barnard.

————. "Dr. Richard Jordan Gatling, Memorial No. 1433." Accessed July 2019. https://www.findagrave.com/memorial/1433/richard-jordan-gatling.

————. "Duncan Dickey, Memorial No. 83160053." Accessed November 2019. https://www.findagrave.com/memorial/83160053/duncan-dickey.

————. "Edna Anna Galt, Memorial No. 16698998." Accessed November 2019. https://www.findagrave.com/memorial/166989980/edna-anna-galt.

————. "Eli Lilly, Memorial No. 1903." Accessed July 2019. https://www.findagrave.com/memorial/1903/eli-lilly.

————. "Elizabeth Anderson Carpenter, Memorial No. 26197134." Accessed August 2019. https://www.findagrave.com/memorial/26197134/elizabeth-carpenter.

————. "Elizabeth Harrison Walker, Memorial No. 198110283." Accessed July 2019. https://www.findagrave.com/memorial/198110283/elizabeth-walker.

————. "Eliza Gregory Patton, Memorial No. 76151484." Accessed October 2019. https://www.findagrave.com/memorial/76151484/eliza-patton.

————. "Elnora Knobloch, Memorial No. 19589759." Accessed September 2019. https://www.findagrave.com/memorial/19589759/elnora-knobloch.

————. "Emily Lemon Lilly, Memorial No. 27387747." Accessed July 2019. https://www.findagrave.com/memorial/27387747/emily-lilly/photo.

————. "Esther Carlson, Memorial No. 123457628." Accessed October 2019. https://www.findagrave.com/memorial/123457628/esther-carlson.

————. "Ewald Cemetery." Accessed September 2019. https://www.findagrave.com/cemetery/2209063/ewald-cemetery.

————. "Floyd E. Pruett, Memorial No. 12819775." Accessed November 2019. https://www.findagrave.com/memorial/12819775/floyd-e-pruett.

————. "Forest Hill Cemetery." Accessed September 2019. https://www.findagrave.com/cemetery/85034/forest-hill-cemetery.

————. "Frances E. 'Fanny' Sullivan, Memorial No. 77007474." Accessed October 2019. https://www.findagrave.com/memorial/77007474/frances-e-sullivan.

————. "George Carpenter, III, Memorial No. 22757657." Accessed August 2019. https://www.findagrave.com/memorial/22757657/george-carpenter.

————. "George Grey Barnard, Memorial No. 10831209." Accessed October 2019. https://www.findagrave.com/memorial/10831209/george-grey-barnard.

————. "Harriet S. Murdock, Memorial No. 34819949." Accessed September 2019. https://www.findagrave.com/memorial/34819949/harriet-s-murdock.

————. "Henrietta "Harriet" Knapp Patton, Memorial No. 75804696." Accessed October 2019. https://www.findagrave.com/memorial/75804696/henrietta-patton.

————. "Henry P. Ewald, Memorial No. 19591642." Accessed September 2019. https://www.findagrave.com/memorial/19591642/henry-p_-ewald.

————. "Hollan Murphy Almon, Memorial No. 17423871." Accessed October 2019. https://www.findagrave.com/memorial/17423871/hollan-almon.

————. "Horace J. Crismond, Memorial No. 34644510." Accessed September 2019. https://www.findagrave.com/memorial/34644510/horace-j-crismond.

————. "Infant Whitlatch, Memorial No. 64363802." Accessed August 2019. https://www.findagrave.com/memorial/64363802/infant-whitlatch.

————. "Irv Rissler "Err" Boone, Memorial No. 13556609." Accessed September 2019. https://www.findagrave.com/memorial/13556609/irv-rissler-boone.

————. "Isaac Himmlbeger, Memorial No. 34776624." Accessed September 2019. https://www.findagrave.com/memorial/34776624/isaac-himmelberger.

————. "James McConnell, Memorial No. 35738789." Accessed October 2019. https://www.findagrave.com/memorial/35738789/james-mcconnell.

————. "James Whitcomb Riley, Memorial No. 873." Accessed July 2019. https://www.findagrave.com/memorial/873/james-whitcomb-riley.

————. "Jennie E. Olsen, Memorial No. 26462336." Accessed October 2019. https://www.findagrave.com/memorial/26462336/jennie-e-olsen.

————. "Jennie Gunness, Memorial No. 122100102." Accessed October 2019. https://www.findagrave.com/memorial/122100102/jennie-gunness.

————. "Jeremiah Sullivan, Memorial No. 35881908." Accessed October 2019. https://www.findagrave.com/memorial/35881908/jeremiah-sullivan.

————. "John A. Banks, Memorial No. 18576599." Accessed August 2019. https://www.findagrave.com/memorial/18576599/john-a_-banks.

————. "John Almon, Memorial No. 17423894." Accessed October 2019. https://www.findagrave.com/memorial/17423894/john-almon.

————. "John Dillinger, Memorial No. 283." Accessed November 2019. https://www.findagrave.com/memorial/283/john-herbert-dillinger.

————. "John G. Heinl, Memorial No. 3773." Accessed June 2019. https://www.findagrave.com/memorial/3773/john-g_-heinl.

————. "John L. Seaton, Memorial No. 43077595." Accessed November 2019. https://www.findagrave.com/memorial/43077595/john-l-seaton.

————. "John Miller, Memorial No. 19583678." Accessed September 2019. https://www.findagrave.com/memorial/19583678/john-miller.

————. "John Tipton, Memorial No. 6349." Accessed September 2019. https://www.findagrave.com/memorial/8349/john-tipton.

————. "Joseph Tillett, Memorial No. 152179905." Accessed August 2019. https://www.findagrave.com/memorial/152179905/joseph-tillett.

————. "Julia Sullivan, Memorial No. 90749808." Accessed October 2019. https://www.findagrave.com/memorial/90749808/julia-sullivan.

————. "Justus Cemetery." Accessed October 2019. https://www.findagrave.com/cemetery/85575/justus-cemetery.

————. "Kathryn Crismond Armacost, Memorial No. 34532484." Accessed September 2019. https://www.findagrave.com/memorial/34532484/kathryn-armacost.

————. "Lillie A. Himmelberger Crismond, Memorial No. 34644512." Accessed September 2019. https://www.findagrave.com/memorial/34644512/lillie-a-crismond.

————. "Lucy B. Sorenson, Memorial No. 110743375." Accessed October 2019. https://www.findagrave.com/memorial/110743375/lucy-b_-sorenson.

————. "Madge Lillian Gunther McDaniel, Memorial No. 36153746." https://www.findagrave.com/memorial/36153746/madge-lillian-mcdaniel.

———. "Mads Detlev Anton Sorenson, Memorial No. 122097766." https://www.findagrave.com/memorial/122097766/mads-detlev_anton-sorenson.

———. "Maria Cynthia Sloane Lilly, Memorial No. 19587141." Accessed July 2019. https://www.findagrave.com/memorial/19587141/maria-cynthia-lilly.

———. "Marvin Eugene Mounce, Memorial No. 31632975." Accessed October 2019. https://www.findagrave.com/memorial/31632957/marvin-eugene-mounce.

———. "Mary Banks Jones, Memorial No. 148794055." Accessed August 2019. https://www.findagrave.com/memorial/148794055/martha-jones.

———. "Mary Elizabeth Warner Hutcheson, Memorial No. 51928819." Accessed September 2019. https://www.findagrave.com/memorial/51928819/mary-elizabeth-hutcheson.

———. "Mary Goit, Memorial No. 46517259." Accessed October 2019. https://www.findagrave.com/memorial/46517259/mary-goit.

———. "Mary Sansum Almon, Memorial No. 17423906." Accessed October 2019. https://www.findagrave.com/memorial/17423906/mary-almon.

———. "Mary Scott Lord Harrison, Memorial No. 22891." Accessed July 2019. https://www.findagrave.com/memorial/22891/mary-scott-harrison.

———. "Mary Scott 'Mamie' Harrison McKee, Memorial No. 6535363." Accessed July 2019. https://www.findagrave.com/memorial/6535363/mary-scott-mckee.

———. "Matilda Boone, Memorial No. 13556618." Accessed September 2019. https://www.findagrave.com/memorial/13556618/matilda-boone.

———. "Matilda Ewald, Memorial No. 19591616." Accessed September 2019. https://www.findagrave.com/memorial/19591616/matilda-ewald.

———. "Matilda Polk Spencer Tipton, Memorial No. 40385969." Accessed September 2019. https://www.findagrave.com/memorial/40385969/matilda-polk-tipton.

———. "Melmoth Boone, Memorial No. 13556624." Accessed September 2019. https://www.findagrave.com/memorial/13556624/melmoth-boone.

———. "Moses Boone, Memorial No. 14784787." Accessed September 2019. https://www.findagrave.com/memorial/14784787/moses-boone.

———. "Mount Hope Cemetery." Accessed September 2019. https://www.findagrave.com/cemetery/86017/mount-hope-cemetery.

————. "Myrtle A. Sorenson, Memorial No. 110743336." Accessed October 2019. https://www.findagrave.com/memorial/110743336/myrtle-a_-sorenson.

————. "Napoleon Collins, Memorial No. 7454954." Accessed October 2019. https://www.findagrave.com/memorial/7454954/napoleon-collins.

————. "Olethia Walls, Memorial No. 129481384." Accessed November 2019. https://www.findagrave.com/memorial/129481384/olethia-walls.

————. "Pearl Bryan, Memorial No. 30686832." Accessed September 2019. https://www.findagrave.com/memorial/30686832/pearl-bryan.

————. "Peter S. Gunness, Memorial No. 26462609." Accessed October 2019. https://www.findagrave.com/memorial/26462609/peter-s-gunness.

————. "Phebe Rissler Boone, Memorial No. 22263783." Accessed September 2019. https://www.findagrave.com/memorial/22263783/phebe-boone.

————. "Phebe Rissler Boone, Memorial No. 9074877." Accessed September 2019. https://www.findagrave.com/memorial/9074877/phebe-boone.

————. "Philip Gunness, Memorial No. 110743447." Accessed November 2019. https://www.findagrave.com/memorial/110743447/philip-gunness.

————. "Pine Lake Cemetery." Accessed October 2019. https://www.findagrave.com/cemetery/86387/pine-lake-cemetery.

————. "Posey Chapel Cemetery." Accessed October 2019. https://www.findagrave.com/cemetery/1791277/posey-chapel-cemetery.

————. "Randolph Hall Hutcheson, Memorial No. 24583247." Accessed September 2019. https://www.findagrave.com/memorial/24583247/randolph-hall-hutcheson.

————. "Ray Lamphere, Memorial No. 112385917." Accessed October 2019. https://www.findagrave.com/memorial/112385917/ray-lamphere.

————. "Reuben Stepp, Memorial No. 9322541." Accessed November 2019. https://www.findagrave.com/memorial/9322541/reuben-stepp.

————. "Reverend John Bond, Memorial No. 8389263." Accessed November 2019. https://www.findagrave.com/memorial/8389263/john-bond.

————. "Russell Benjamin Harrison, Memorial No. 19504719." Accessed July 2019. https://www.findagrave.com/memorial/19504719/russell-benjamin-harrison.

————. "Samuel Bridgewater, Memorial No. 29956672." Accessed August 2019. https://www.findagrave.com/memorial/29956672/samuel-bridgewater.

———. "Sarah McConnell Banks, Memorial No. 13608899." https://www.findagrave.com/memorial/13608899/sarah-banks.

———. "Sir Malcom Dunbar Hacker, Memorial No. 30855113." Accessed November 2019. https://www.findagrave.com/memorial/30855113/malcome-dunbar-hacker.

———. "Skiles Edward Test, Memorial No. 12966." Accessed February 2020. https://www.findagrave.com/memorial/12966/skiles-edward-test.

———. "Springdale Cemetery." Accessed November 2019. https://www.findagrave.com/cemetery/86990/springdale-cemetery.

———. "Squire Boone, Memorial No. 25701538." Accessed September 2019. https://www.findagrave.com/memorial/25701538/squire-boone.

———. "Stepp Cemetery." Accessed November 2019. https://www.findagrave.com/cemetery/87026/stepp-cemetery.

———. "Susannah "Susan" Boone Rissler, Memorial No. 6273771." Accessed September 2019. https://www.findagrave.com/memorial/6273771/susannah-rissler.

———. "Theodosia Russell Darling, Memorial No. 51588534." Accessed October 2019. https://www.findagrave.com/memorial/51588534/theodesia-darling.

———. "Thomas A. Stepp, Memorial No. 30850294." Accessed November 2019. https://www.findagrave.com/memorial/30850294/thomas-a_-stepp.

———. "Tillett Cemetery." Accessed August 2019. https://www.findagrave.com/cemetery/2169523/tillet-cemetery.

———. "Tommy Thevenow, Memorial No.13789703." Accessed October 2019. https://www.findagrave.com/memorial/13789703/tommy-thevenow.

———. "Wightman Goit, Memorial No. 46515683." Accessed October 2019. https://www.findagrave.com/memorial/46515683/wightman-goit.

———. "William J. Whitlatch, Memorial No. 64363795." Accessed August 2019. https://www.findagrave.com/memorial/64363795/william-j_-whitlatch.

———. "William Owens Murdock, Memorial No. 34819956." Accessed September 2019. https://www.findagrave.com/memorial/34819956/william-owens-murdock.

ABOUT THE AUTHOR

Ashley Hood is the owner and tour guide of Tell-Tale Tours, a haunted history walking tour business in her hometown of Terre Haute, Indiana. She has been fascinated with the history of haunted locations and the "things that go bump in the night" since early childhood, exploring local cemeteries and haunted bridges in rural Indiana as a teenager. In the years since, Ashley has conducted paranormal investigations throughout the midwestern United States, visiting some of the Midwest's most haunted sites. She is a collector of all things macabre and unusual and loves to visit bizarre and unique locations. Ashley is the co-host of *Strange Journeys*, a podcast exploring the darker side of travel. She resides in Terre Haute, Indiana, with a family of fur babies, and, yes, she is a crazy cat lady.

Visit us at
www.historypress.com